ビジネスで
Eメール
すぐに使える
英語表現集

ディー・オー・エム・フロンティア＋
味園真紀＋小林知子──著

Useful expressions
Please let us know by e-mail.
Could you please e-mail us your manual as a PDF file?
Thank you for your e-mail of September 12th.
Could you e-mail us your price quote as soon as possible?
Please e-mail us information concerning your services.
・・・

仕事のEメール
完全版
会社で使うホームページサンプル
＆
組み合わせ自在の応用表現

ベレ出版

# はじめに

ここ数年のビジネスにおける最も大きい変化のひとつに、Eメールの普及があげられます。以前は、海外とのやりとりは手紙と電話が中心でしたが、最近ではEメールの普及により手紙がEメールに取って代わり、時差を気にしなくてもよいことから、電話さえもEメールに変わりつつあります。

Eメールは、手紙のように投函してから相手に届くまでに時間がかかることなく、瞬時に送受信ができるので、便利になった一方、読んで見てすぐに返信しなければならないなど、ビジネスにスピードを求められるようになりました。

従来の英文ビジネスレターでは、格式が重んじられ、格調高い表現が好まれましたが、スピードや簡潔さを求めるEメールでは、相手にとって読みやすく、理解しやすい内容にまとめることが大切です。

1日に100通以上のメールを処理している人も少なくない中、メールが長々と読みにくいために後回しにされたり、放置されたりすることのないよう、シンプルで、言いたいことが相手に伝わりやすい文章を書くよう、心がけましょう。

本書では、皆さんが必要とされる表現が引きやすいように、よく使うビジネス英語表現を様々なビジネスシーンにわけ、さらにその中を詳細シーン・機能別にまとめています。必要な部分を組み合わせて使ってください。

また、Ⅲでは、ホームページを英語で作るとき、また英語のホームページをご覧になるときに役立つ表現をまとめています。ホームページを開設している方は、ぜひ英語サイトも作ってみてはいかがでしょうか。

2003年9月

株式会社ディー・オー・エム・フロンティア

味園　真紀

小林　知子

# CONTENTS

## Ⅰ．Eメールの書き方とルール

# Ⅱ. 機能別Eメールサンプル・表現集

# Ⅲ. ホームページでよく使う表現

# Ⅳ．すぐに役立つ会社の資料

コラム

# I

# Eメールの書き方とルール

# 1 Eメールのフォーマット

## （Eメールのレイアウトサンプル）

Date:September 15, 2003 ·························· ①
To:brian@abc.com ······························ ②
From: watanabe@asahi.co.jp ···················· ③
Subject: New e-mail add. ······················ ④

Dear Brian: ·································· ⑤

Effective from October 14th, my new e-mail address ⎫
will be: mwatanabe@asahi.co.jp             ⎬ ⑥

Best Regards, ·································· ⑦

Maki Watanabe ⎫
Overseas Sales Division
ASAHI Co., Ltd.
1-2-3 Nishi-Shinjuku, Shinjuku-ku, Tokyo 345-6789 ⎬ ⑧
Phone +81-3-1234-5678
Fax +81-3-1234-5679
E-mail: watanabe@asahi.co.jp
Web: http://www.asahi.co.jp ⎭

①**日　付**（自動的に発信されます）

②**受信者のアドレス**（必要に応じてCC／BCC欄も使用）

③**発信者のアドレス**（登録されているアドレスが自動的に発信されます）

④**件　名**

Subject：欄（返信のときはRe:欄）に件名を記載します。

件名を見て、内容の重要度が判断されますので、具体的で分かりやすい件名にしましょう。

「4．Eメールの件名サンプル」で、よく使う件名の例をまとめましたので、ご参照ください。

⑤**敬　辞**

Dear Mr.（Ms.）ラストネーム：が一般的です。

ある程度親しい場合は、Dear ファーストネーム：を使用します。

「ご担当者様」など、相手の名前が特定できない場合は、Dear Sir/Madam: を使用します。

⑥**本　文**

正式なビジネスレターよりも簡潔に記載します。

本文は、改行や段落分けをするなどして、相手が読みやすいように配慮しましょう。

⑦**結　辞**

Sincerely, やBest Regards, が一般的です。

Thank you.もよく使います。

⑧**署　名**

Eメールの機能で署名欄をつくることができます。

署名欄には、氏名、役職名、部署名、会社名、電話番号、FAX番号、Eメー

ルアドレス、ホームページアドレスなどから必要なものを記載します。

## ⑨その他

間違ったアドレスにEメールが送信される事を想定して、最後に次のような
文章を入れている企業もよく見られます。

The information in this e-mail and any attachments is confidential and intended only for the use of the individual(s) to whom it is addressed. If you are not a named addressee or otherwise an intended recipient, you are requested to immediately notify the sender and to delete this e-mail and all attachments from your system.

（訳）

本メールや添付物にある情報は機密であり、宛てられた個人のみの利用を意図しています。あなたが宛名と違う場合や意図された受取人でない場合は、速やかに送信者に連絡し、本メールや添付物をシステムから削除してください。

# 2 Eメールのルール

## （1）メッセージは簡潔に、必要な事柄のみを重要なものから書く。

相手が読んですぐに理解できるように、できるだけ短くシンプルな文章にします。

時候の挨拶や、社交辞令などは一切不要です。

ただし、親しい場合はコミュニケーションとして、ある程度の近況報告などは入れるとよいでしょう。

## （2）冗長的な表現はしない。

例） make a decision → decide

give a response → respond

in receipt of → received

as to → about

with regard to → about

due to the fact that → because

prior to → before

## （3）簡単な単語・表現を使う。

（2）と同様、読みやすさを重視しますので、できるだけ簡単な単語・表現を使いましょう。

例） sufficient → enough

eliminate → remove

obtain → get

## （4）読みやすいレイアウトにする。

受信者の1行文字数と発信者の1行文字数が異なる場合があります。

受信者の1行文字数の方が少ない場合、レイアウトがくずれ、読みにくくなります。適当な長さで改行し、段落分けをしましょう。

## （5）読み手中心の文章を書く。

従来のビジネスレターと同様、読み手中心の文章を書くように心がけましょう。

## （6）あいまいな表現をさけ、明確に。

日付などはなるべく具体的に記載します。

例）✕ Please let me know the delivery date.

（納品日を知らせてください）

○ Please let me know the delivery date by October 5th.

（納品日を10月5日までに知らせてください）

## （7）すべて大文字、小文字でタイプしない。

すべて大文字の文章やすべて小文字の文章は、読みづらいばかりか、相手に対して失礼です。

## （8）顔文字を乱用しない。

顔文字はビジネスメールには不適切です。

#  3 Eメールで使う省略語

| | | |
|---|---|---|
| REQ＝Request | （依頼） |
| Re＝Regarding | （〜の件） |
| info＝information | （情報） |
| FYI＝For your information | （ご参考までに） |
| TYIA＝Thank you in advance | （よろしくお願いします） |
| ASAP＝as soon as possible | （できるだけ早く） |
| thru＝through | （通して） |
| pls＝please | （どうぞ） |
| b/w＝between | （〜の間） |
| w/＝with | （〜と） |
| w/o＝without | （〜なしで） |
| Div＝Division | （事業部） |
| Dept＝Department | （部） |
| Sect＝Section | （課） |

その他、Jan＝January（1月）などの月や、Mon＝Monday（月曜日）などの曜日も省略形を用いることもできますが、ビジネスメールでは、一般的に省略形は用いません［May（5月）には省略形はありません］。

日付の表記は、正式にはJanuary 1st、2nd、3rd、4th …となりますが、EメールではJanuary 1、2、3、4 …と省略して書かれることも多いです。正式な表記方法の方が相手にフォーマルな印象を与えます。

# 4　Eメールの件名サンプル

よく使う件名のサンプルをまとめました。

## ◇問い合わせ

| | |
|---|---|
| 問い合わせ | Inquiry |
| NK-3プリンタに関する問い合わせ | Inquiry about the NK-3 printer |
| 資料請求 | Information request |
| 質問 | Question |
| ちょっとした質問 | Quick question |
| 貴社の新製品に関する質問 | Question about your new products |

## ◇依頼

| | |
|---|---|
| 依頼 | Request（=REQ） |
| 情報依頼 | Request for information |
| 製品カタログ依頼 | Request for product catalog |
| 許可願い | Request for permission |
| アポイントメント | Appointment |

## ◇通知・お知らせ

| | |
|---|---|
| お知らせ | Announcement |
| Eメールアドレス | My e-mail address |
| Eメールアドレスの変更 | Change of e-mail address |
| 住所変更 | Change of our address |
| 移転します | We're moving |
| 営業時間の変更 | Change in business hours |
| 休暇 | Vacation |
| 異動 | Relocation |
| 転勤になります | I'll be transferred |

| | |
|---|---|
| 戻りました | I'm back |
| 情報 | Information |
| 通知 | Notice |

## ◇返信

| | |
|---|---|
| 貴殿のEメール | Your e-mail |
| 貴殿のファックス | Your fax |
| 1月5日付けの貴書 | Your letter of Jan. 5 |
| 貴殿のご依頼 | Your request |

## ◇見積り

| | |
|---|---|
| 見積り | Price quote / Quotation / Estimate |
| K-02型ノート型パソコンの見積り | Quotation for the K-02 laptop computer |

## ◇注文

| | |
|---|---|
| 注文 | Order |
| 急ぎの注文 | Rush order |
| K-02型ノート型パソコンの注文 | Order for the K-02 laptop computer |
| 注文番号0001 | P.O. No. 0001 |
| 注文番号0001の変更 | Change in our order No. 0001 |
| 注文番号0001の取消し | Cancellation of our order No. 0001 |

## ◇請求

| | |
|---|---|
| 請求書 | Invoice |
| 請求書番号0001の支払いについて | Your payment for invoice No. 0001 |

## ◇出荷

| | |
|---|---|
| 出荷予定 | Shipping schedule |
| 注文番号0001の出荷 | Shipment for your order No. 0001 |

## ◇出張

| | |
|---|---|
| 1月の貴社訪問 | My visit in Jan. |
| ボストンへの出張 | My trip to Boston |
| 5月15日の予定 | My schedule on May 15 |
| 日程表 | Itinerary |

## ◇確認

| | |
|---|---|
| 貴殿の日本滞在の手配 | Arrangements for your stay in Japan |
| 予約の確認 | Confirmation of reservation |
| 承認 | Approval |

## ◇苦情・クレーム

| | |
|---|---|
| 不良品 | Defective goods |
| 品違い | Wrong product |
| 請求書番号001の間違い | Error in invoice No. 001 |
| 出荷遅れ | Delayed shipment |

## ◇お礼

| | |
|---|---|
| ありがとうございます | Thank you |
| ご助力、ありがとうございます | Thank you for your help |
| データをありがとうございました | Thank you for the data |
| Eメールをありがとうございました | Thank you for your e-mail |

## ◇お祝い

| | |
|---|---|
| おめでとう！ | Congratulations! |
| 昇進おめでとう！ | Congratulations on your promotion! |
| 結婚おめでとう！ | Congratulations on your marriage! |

## ◇謝罪

| | |
|---|---|
| お詫び | Apology |
| 不良品に対するお詫び | Apology for the defective products |

| | |
|---|---|
| ごめんなさい | Sorry |

◇**お悔やみ・お見舞い**

| | |
|---|---|
| お悔やみ | Condolences |
| 早くよくなってください | Get well soon |
| ご自愛ください | Take care of yourself |

◇**挨拶**

| | |
|---|---|
| 季節のご挨拶！ | Season's Greetings! |
| こんにちは | Hello |
| 元気ですか | How are you? |

◇**その他**

| | |
|---|---|
| 至急 | Urgent |
| 重要 | Important |
| 報告書 | Report |
| 招待 | Invitation |
| 月例営業会議 | Monthly sales meeting |
| 夏のキャンペーン | Summer campaign |
| 添付ファイル | Attachment |

# Ⅱ

## 機能別Eメールサンプル・表現集

# 1 社外ビジネスメール

## 1. 資料請求・問い合わせ

### ①資料請求・問い合わせ

資料の請求や問い合わせのメールには、自己紹介、相手をどのようにして知ったか、問い合わせ内容などを記載します。

---

Subject: Request for the information about your new products

Dear Sir/Madam:

We visited your web site, and are very interested in your new products.
We would like to receive the latest information about your new products by e-mail.
My e-mail address is misono@abc.co.jp
We look forward to hearing from you.

Sincerely,

---

件名：貴社の新製品に関する資料請求

ご担当者様

貴社のホームページを拝見し、新商品に非常に関心をもちました。
新商品についての最新の資料をEメールにてお送りいただければ幸いです。
私のアドレスは、misono@abc.co.jpです。
ご連絡をお待ちしております。

## Words and Phrases

| | |
|---|---|
| □会社案内 | company brochure／company profile |
| □製品カタログ | product catalog |
| □製品リスト | product list |
| □サービスリスト | service list |
| □価格表 | price list |
| □資料、情報 | information |
| □無料サンプル | free sample |
| □仕様書 | specifications |
| □〜に関心がある、〜に興味がある | be interested in 〜 |
| □〜を1部 | a copy of 〜 |
| □ありがたく思う、感謝する | appreciate |

## Useful Expressions
### 応用表現

### 自己紹介する

□弊社は、東京でもっとも成功しているコンサルティング会社のひとつです。
We are one of the most successful consulting companies in Tokyo.

□弊社は、日本でもっとも先進的なウェブデザイン会社のひとつです。
We are one of the leading web design companies in Japan.

□私は、翻訳会社で秘書として勤務しています。
I work for a translation company as a secretary.

□私は、DOMF社国際営業部に勤務しています。
I work in the International Sales Department of DOMF Corporation.

□本日のXY新聞にて、貴社の広告を拝見しました。

We read your advertisement in today's XY newspaper.

□XY Magazineの最新号で、貴社の広告を拝見しました。

I saw your advertisement in the current issue of XY Magazine.

□XY Magazineの9月号で、貴社の広告を拝見しました。

I saw your advertisement in the September issue of XY Magazine.

□貴社の製品カタログを拝見する機会がありました。

I had an opportunity to see your product catalog.

□ABC社の田中氏より、貴社のコンサルティングサービスを紹介していただきました。

Mr. Tanaka of ABC Corporation referred your consulting service to us.

□貴社はカリフォルニア最大手の通信販売会社だと伺っております。

We understand that you are the leading mail-order company in California.

□貴社のソフトウェアの価格を知りたいのです。

We would like to know the prices of your software.

□貴社の新製品について、もっと知りたいのです。

We would like to know more about your new products.

□A-35型コンピュータ100台の在庫はありますか。

Do you have one hundred of the A-35 computers in stock?

□この製品と旧型製品の一番大きな違いは何ですか。

What is the biggest difference between this product and its older version?

□貴社のコーヒー豆の輸入に非常に関心があります。

We are very interested in importing your coffee beans.

□貴社の色揃えについて知りたいのです。

We would like to know what selection of colors you offer.

### 資料などを請求する

□製品カタログを送っていただけますか。

Could you please send us a product catalog?

□会社案内を下記の住所に送付してください。

Please send your company brochure to the address below:

□製品カタログを航空郵便で送ってください。

Please send your product catalog by airmail.

□価格表をファックスしてください。

Please fax us your price list.

□貴社のサービスに関する情報をEメールで送ってください。

Please e-mail us information concerning your services.

□可能であれば、貴社の価格表をEメールの添付ファイルで送っていただけませんか。

Could you send us your price list via e-mail as an attachment, if possible?

□本製品に関して、どのような情報でもいただけると助かります。

It would be helpful if you could give us any information about the product.

□関連資料をお送りください。

Please send us any relevant information.

□PDFファイルのマニュアルをEメールで送っていただけますか。

Could you please e-mail us your manual as a PDF file?

□サービス一覧表を送っていただければ幸いです。

I would appreciate it if you could send us your service list.

□無料サンプルを、次の住所まで送っていただけませんか。

Would it be possible for you to send a free sample to the following address?

□misono@abc.co.jpまでお返事ください。

Please respond to misono@abc.co.jp

□Eメールでお知らせください。

Please let us know by e-mail.

□ファックスでお知らせください。

Please let us know by fax.

□下記のアドレスまでEメールをください。

Please e-mail us at the following address:

□03-1234-5678までお電話ください。

Please call us at 03-1234-5678.

□ご連絡をお待ちしております。

I look forward to hearing from you.

□早速お返事いただければ幸いです。

We would appreciate a prompt reply.

□5月30日までにお返事いただければ幸いです。

We would appreciate your reply by May 30th.

□カタログをいただけるのを楽しみにしています。

We look forward to receiving the catalog.

□よろしくお願いいたします（前もって御礼申し上げます）。

Thank you in advance.

# ②資料請求・問い合わせに対する返事

資料請求や問い合わせに対する返事では、問い合わせに対する感謝の意や送付資料の内容について述べます。最後に、相手の要求に応えるよう努力する旨や、検討をお願いする旨を述べましょう。

---

Subject: Re: Request for the information about your new products

Dear Mr. Jones:

Thank you for your inquiry about our new products.
The attached file is the product catalog.

If you need further information, please feel free to contact us.
We are looking forward to hearing from you.

Sincerely,

---

件名：Re：貴社の新製品に関する資料請求

ジョーンズ様

弊社の新製品に関してお問い合わせいただき、ありがとうございます。
添付したファイルは製品カタログです。

さらに情報が必要であれば、お気軽にご連絡ください。
ご連絡をお待ちしております。

---

## Words and Phrases

| | |
|---|---|
| □問い合わせ | inquiry |
| □関心、興味 | interest |
| □連絡する | contact |
| □～でご連絡ください | contact me by ～ |
| □ご検討用に | for your review |
| □ご参考に | for your information |
| □お気軽に～してください | please feel free to ～ |
| □ご遠慮なく～してください | please do not hesitate to ～ |
| □現在は | currently |

## Useful Expressions
## 応用表現

問い合わせに対して感謝の意を述べる

□ご関心をお寄せいただき、ありがとうございます。

Thank you for your interest.

□弊社の製品にご関心をお寄せいただき、ありがとうございます。

Thank you for your interest in our products.

□新製品に関するお問い合わせのファックスをいただき、ありがとうございます。

Thank you for your fax of inquiry regarding our new product.

□弊社のメンテナンスサービスに関するお問い合わせをいただき、ありがとうございます。

Thank you for your inquiry about our maintenance service.

□お問い合わせいただき光栄です。

We are pleased to receive your inquiry.

□弊社の新製品に関するお問い合わせをいただき、ありがとうございます。

Thank you for your inquiry regarding our new product.

□お問い合わせに感謝いたします。
We appreciate your inquiry.

□9月12日付けのEメールをいただき、ありがとうございます。
Thank you for your e-mail of September 12th.

＊"I appreciate ～"は、"Thank you for ～"より丁寧な表現です。

□ご請求いただきました製品カタログと価格表をお送りいたします。
We are pleased to send you our product catalog and price list that you requested.

□製品のサンプルを航空便でお送りいたします。
We will send a product sample by airmail.

□最新の価格表を添付いたします。
We are attaching the latest price list.

□ご請求いただきました製品カタログを5部発送いたしました。
We have mailed five copies of the product catalog that you requested.

□ご請求いただきました情報をファックスでお送りいたします。
I will fax you the information that you requested.

□申し訳ございませんが、製品のサンプルをお送りすることができません。
We regret that we cannot send you product samples.

□XY-IIのサンプルをお送りできます。
We can send a sample of the XY-II.

□現在、お送りできる資料がありません。
We do not have any information to send you at this time.

□現在、英語版の会社案内を用意しておりません。
The English version of our company brochure is not currently available.

□製品カタログをPDF形式でご提供しております。
　We provide our product catalog in PDF format.

□このページをご覧になるには、アクロバットリーダーが必要です。
　You need Acrobat Reader to view this page.

## 在庫状況について応える

□まだたくさん在庫がございます。
　We still have plenty in stock.

□ABCソフトウェア100個は、すぐに出荷可能です。
　We can ship 100 ABC software immediately.

□ご依頼いただいた製品は、ただいま在庫を切らしております。
　The product you requested is currently out of stock.

□お問い合わせの製品は、数に限りがございます。
　We have a limited supply of the product you inquired about.

## その他の問い合わせに応える

□申し訳ございませんが、現在、私どものホームページは日本語のみとなっております。
　I am sorry, but our web site is currently in Japanese only.

□海外に代理店はありません。
　We do not have any agencies overseas.

□ニューヨークの代理店からすぐに連絡が行くはずです。
　You should hear from our agency in New York shortly.

□あなたの質問にすぐにはお答えできかねます。
　We cannot answer your question at this time.

□お調べしてお返事いたします。
　I will look into your inquiry and get back to you.

## その他・結びの挨拶

□ご注文をお待ちしております。

We look forward to receiving an order from you.

□何かご質問がございましたらご遠慮なくお問い合わせください。

If you have any questions, please feel free to contact us.

□他に資料が必要な場合は、ご遠慮なく03-9876-5432または
sakura@aaa.co.jp までご連絡ください。

If you need additional information, please don't hesitate to contact
me at 03-9876-5432   or  sakura@aaa.co.jp

□弊社のホームページのURLは、http://www.abc.co.jpです。

The URL of our web site is http://www.abc.co.jp

□私共のサービスがお役に立てば幸いです。

I hope you will find our service helpful.

□お問い合わせに重ねて御礼申し上げます。

Thank you again for your inquiry.

---

**【Eメールアドレスとホームページアドレスの記載方法】**

Eメールアドレスやホームページアドレスが文末に記載される場合は、正確なアドレスを伝えるために（アドレスの最後にはピリオドがないため）、文末のピリオドを打たないか、アドレスを＜＞で括って＜＞の外にピリオドを打ちます。

（Eメールアドレスの例）
○My e-mail address is ohtsuka@abc.co.jp
○My e-mail address is <ohtsuka@abc.co.jp>.

（ホームページアドレスの例）
○Please visit our web site: http://www.abc.com
○Please visit our web site: <http://www.abc.com>.

# ③資料請求・問い合わせに対する返事をした後のフォローアップ

資料を送付しても注文などの反応がない場合は、資料が届いたかどうかの確認を兼ねてフォローしましょう。

Subject: Did you get our product catalog?

Dear Mr. Jones:

I hope you received our product catalog.
If you need any other information, please feel free to contact us.

We look forward to hearing from you.

Sincerely,

件名：弊社の製品カタログ受け取られましたでしょうか

ジョーンズ様

弊社の製品カタログを受け取られたことと存じます。
他に必要な資料がございましたら、ご遠慮なくご連絡ください。

ご連絡をお待ちしております。

## Words and Phrases

| | |
|---|---|
| □受け取る | receive |
| □〜かなと思う | wonder |
| □追加資料 | additional information |
| □ご要望がございましたら | at your request |
| □喜んで〜する | be happy to 〜 |

## Useful Expressions
### 応用表現

**資料や返事が受け取られているか確認する**

□弊社のカタログを受け取られたことと存じます。
I hope you received our catalog.

□SKINCAREの無料サンプルを受け取られましたでしょうか。
We wondered whether you received a free sample of SKINCARE.

**商品や自社をアピールする**

□弊社の製品は、若い女性に大変人気がございます。
Our products are very popular among young ladies.

□数多くの建設会社をご支援してまいりました。
We have successfully assisted a number of construction companies.

**今後の対応について述べる**

□無料サンプルを差し上げております。
We can offer you a free sample.

□喜んで、簡単な実演の手配をさせていただきます。
We would be happy to arrange a brief demonstration for you.

□喜んで、私どもの新製品の特徴をご説明させていただきます。

We would be happy to explain the features of our new products.

□貴社とお仕事をさせていただく可能性について話し合えれば幸いです。

We would be pleased to discuss the possibility of working with you.

□ご要望がございましたら、追加の資料をお送りいたします。

We will send you additional information at your request.

□私どもの製品について何かご質問がございましたら、喜んでお答えいたします。

If you have any questions about our products, we would be happy to answer your questions.

□弊社ウェブサイトにて新製品をご覧いただけます。

You can view our new product on our web site.

□さらに情報をお求めであれば、（012）345-6789までお電話いただくか、info@abc.comまでＥメールにてお問い合わせください。

For more information, please call us at (012)345-6789, or e-mail us at info@abc.com

□近々、貴社とお取り引きできれば幸いです。

We look forward to doing business with you in the near future.

# ２．見積り・交渉

## ①見積り・提案書の依頼

考慮してほしい具体的な条件がすでにある場合は、その条件のもとに見積もってもらうよう依頼します。

---

Subject: About your P-XY computers

Dear Sir/Madam:

We visited your web site yesterday, and would like to buy some P-XY computers.
We would like to know its wholesale price and the minimum order.

We look forward to hearing from you.

Sincerely,

---

件名：貴社のP-XY型コンピュータに関して

ご担当者様

昨日貴社のホームページを拝見し、P-XY型コンピュータを数台購入したいと考えています。
卸売価格とその最低注文台数を知りたいのです。

お返事をお待ちしております。

## Words and Phrases

| | |
|---|---|
| □ 見積り | price quote／quote／quotation |
| □ ～の見積り | price quote for ～ |
| □ 見積もる | quote |
| □ 確定見積り | firm price quote |
| □ オファー、提案 | offer |
| □ 品目 | item |
| □ 数量 | quantity |
| □ 仕様 | specifications |
| □ 納期 | delivery date／date of delivery |
| □ 取引条件 | terms and conditions |
| □ 引渡条件 | delivery terms |
| □ 支払条件 | payment terms |
| □ 希望の～ | required ～ |
| □ ボリュームディスカウント | volume discount |
| □ 価格 | price |
| □ 卸売価格 | wholesale price |
| □ 最低注文数 | the minimum order |
| □ 最低価格 | the lowest price |
| □ 購入する | buy／purchase |

## Useful Expressions
### 応用表現

**見積り依頼の理由を述べる**

□貴社の新製品に関心があります。

We are interested in your new products.

□貴社の文書管理ソフトの購入を検討しています。

We are considering purchasing your document management software.

□貴社のコンサルティングサービスの独創性にとても感銘を受けました。
We are very impressed with the originality of your consulting services.

□ABC Magazineにて、貴社の広告と、貴社社長のインタビュー記事を拝見しました。
We saw your advertisement and the article of an interview of your president in ABC Magazine.

## 見積りを依頼する

□カリフォルニアワイン1,000本の価格を見積もっていただきたいのですが。
We would like your quote for 1,000 bottles of California wine.

□次の品目に対して、価格を見積もってください。
Please quote a price on the following items:

□できるだけ早く、Eメールで見積りを送っていただけませんか。
Could you e-mail us your price quote as soon as possible?

□7月2日までにXY-A型冷蔵庫50台の見積りをEメールで送ってください。
Please e-mail us a quote for 50 XY-A refrigerators by July 2nd.

□8月15日までに見積りが必要です。
We need a price quote by August 15th.

□見積りをファックスにてお送りください。
Please send us a price quote by fax.

□最低価格で見積もってください。
Please quote the lowest price.

□最も安い価格で見積もっていただけますか。
Would you kindly quote your best price?

## その他・結びの挨拶

□大量注文したいと思っています。
We will place a large order.

□定期的に注文したいと思っています。

We will place regular orders.

□価格が他社に負けないものであれば、すぐに発注します。

If your prices are competitive, we will place an order with you soon.

□支払条件も提示してください。

Please indicate the payment terms as well.

□納期をお知らせください。

Please inform us of your delivery date.

□お見積りをお待ちしております。

We look forward to receiving your quote.

□ご提案をお待ちしております。

We look forward to receiving your offer.

# ②見積り・提案書の提示

見積り条件がある場合は、その条件を考慮して見積もります。
ボリュームディスカウントなどがある場合は、その旨も伝えましょう。

Subject: Re: About your P-XY computers

Dear Mr. Jones:

Thank you for your inquiry.
Yes, we can offer you US$80 per unit as a wholesale price, and the minimum order must be 100.

If you have any questions, please don't hesitate to contact us at kobayashi@abc.com
We look forward to your order.

Sincerely,

---

件名：Re: 貴社のP-XY型コンピュータに関して

ジョーンズ様

お問い合わせいただき、ありがとうございます。
卸売価格として、1台US$80でご提供できますが、最低注文数は100台です。

何かご質問がございましたら、kobayashi@abc.comまでご遠慮なくお問い合わせください。
ご注文をお待ちしております。

| | |
|---|---|
| □提案する | offer |
| □単価 | unit price／price per unit |
| □合計金額 | total price |
| □特別価格 | special price |
| □割引き | discount／reduction in price |
| □航空便で | by air |
| □船便で | by sea／by surface |
| □運賃 | shipping fee |
| □為替手形 | draft |
| □税込 | including tax |
| □税別 | without tax |
| □添付する | attach |
| □添付 | attachment |
| □喜んで〜する | be pleased to 〜 |
| □〜より多くの | more than 〜 |
| □〜より少ない | less than 〜 |
| □〜以上 ⇔ 〜以下 | 〜 or more ⇔ 〜 or less |

## Useful Expressions
### 応用表現

**見積書などを提出する**

□見積書を添付いたします。

Attached is our quotation.

□下記の通り、お見積もり申し上げます。

We are pleased to quote as follows:

□下記の通り、ご提案申し上げます。

We are pleased to provide you an offer as follows:

42

□Y-1型スキャナの見積書をお送りいたします。

We are pleased to send you our price quote for the Y-1 scanners.

□仕様書も添付いたします。

We will attach the specifications as well.

## 価格について述べる

□消費税は価格に含まれています。

Tax is included in the price.

□消費税は価格に含まれていません。

Tax is not included in the price.

□この価格は税別です。

This price is without tax.

□本見積り価格は、本船渡し価格です。

The quoted price is FOB.

□最も低い見積り価格をご提示しています。

We have quoted the lowest possible price.

## 値引きについて述べる

□特別価格でご提供させていただきます。

We would like to offer you a special price.

□初めてのご注文の場合には、10%の特別値引きをいたします。

Your initial order qualifies for a special discount of 10%.

□50台以上ご注文いただければ、値引きさせていただきます。

An order of 50 units or more will receive a discount.

□100個以上のご注文は割引対象となります。

An order of 100 or more is eligible to receive a discount.

□20個以上のご注文につきましては、見積りより15％引きの特別価格でご提供します。

For quantities of 20 or more, there is a special 15% discount on the prices quoted.

□この値引きは、注文数によります。

This discount depends on the size of the order.

## その他の条件について述べる

□支払条件は相談に応じます。

We would like to discuss the payment terms.

□分割払いが可能です。

You may pay in installments.

□契約金をいただきます。

The price of the contract deposit has to be paid.

□2003年10月5日頃の納品となります。

Our target delivery date is October 5th, 2003.

## その他・結びの挨拶

□1個よりご注文を承っております。

Our minimum order is one.

□本見積りは、2003年12月15日まで有効です。

This price quote expires on December 15th, 2003.

□貴社からのご注文をお待ちしております。

We look forward to your order.

□貴社からの初のご注文をお待ちしております。

We look forward to your first order.

□貴社のお役に立てることを楽しみにしております。

We look forward to being of service to you.

# ③見積り・提案書受領後の交渉

提示された見積りや提案書に納得がいかない場合は交渉します。まずは、相手に交渉の余地の有無を尋ね、どのような条件なら交渉できるのかを尋ねます。

---

Subject: Request for discount

Dear Ms. Smith:

Thank you for your offer of March 7th.
However, we find the price is too high.
Another company offers similar products at US$70 per unit.
If you could take an additional 10% off the price, we would like to place an order with you soon.

Do you think you could reconsider?
Thank you.

---

件名：値引きのお願い

スミス様

3月7日付けのオファーをいただき、ありがとうございました。
価格が高すぎると思います。
他社が、類似品を1台US$70で提供しています。
もう10％値引きしていただければ、すぐに貴社に発注いたします。

もう一度ご検討いただけますか。
よろしくお願いいたします。

## Useful Expressions
### 応用表現

### 見積りの受領を伝える

□見積りを送っていただき、ありがとうございました。

Thank you for sending us your quotation.

□2月1日付けの見積りを受領いたしました。

We received your quotation dated February 1st.

### 交渉する

□次の条件をご検討ください。

Please examine the following terms:

### 【注文数】
□最低注文数が多すぎます。

The minimum order is too large.

□最低注文数を減らしていただけますか。

Could you reduce the minimum order?

### 【価格】
□思っていたより価格が高いです。

The price is higher than we expected.

□私どももっと低価格を期待していました。

We expected a better price.

□10％値引きしていただけますか。

Could you give us a price reduction of 10%?

□もう5％値引きしていただけませんか。

Could you give us an additional 5% discount?

□5％値引きしていただけるようでしたら、発注しようと思います。

We will place an order if you reduce the price by 5%.

□FOB価格ではなく、CIF価格でお願いしたいのですが。

We would like to know the CIF price instead of the FOB price.

## 【支払条件】

□支払条件を変更してください。

Please change the payment terms.

□支払条件だけは承諾できかねます。

Only the payment terms are not acceptable.

□ 毎月の支払いでなく、3分割払いにしていただけるか知りたいのですが。

We would like to know if you could allow us to make the payment in three installments instead of monthly payments.

## 【納期】

□納期を変更していただきたいのです。

We would like to have the delivery date changed.

□納期を早めていただくことは可能ですか。

Is it possible to expedite the delivery date?

## その他・結びの挨拶

□次の条件を承諾していただけると信じております。

We believe the following terms will be acceptable to you.

□低価格を提示していただくための条件を教えていただけますか。

Could you tell me your conditions for a lower price?

## ④見積り・提案書を承諾する

交渉内容が受諾できるものであれば、その旨を伝えます。

---

Subject: Re: Request for discount

Dear Mr. Jones:

We have agreed with your counteroffer of January 20th requesting a reduction in price.
We can offer you an additional 10% reduction in price.

If you have any questions, please feel free to contact us.
Thank you for your business.

Sincerely,

---

件名：Re:値引きのお願い

ジョーンズ様

1月20日付けの、値引き依頼のカウンターオファーを承諾いたします。
さらに10％値引きさせていただきます。

何かご質問がございましたら、お気軽にお問い合わせください。
お取り引きいただき、ありがとうございます。

## Words and Phrases

| | |
|---|---|
| □〜に同意する | agree with 〜 |
| □受け入れる／受諾する | accept |
| □〜という条件で | on condition that 〜 |

## Useful Expressions

### 応用表現

**カウンターオファーを承諾する**

□3月1日付けのカウンターオファーを承諾いたしました。
We have agreed with your counteroffer of March 1st.

□5月5日付けの貴社からのカウンターオファーを喜んで承諾いたします。
We are pleased to accept your counteroffer dated May 5th.

□値引き依頼のカウンターオファーを承諾いたしました。
Your counteroffer requesting a reduction in price has been accepted.

□今回のご注文について、さらに5%の値引きをさせていただきます。
We can offer you an extra discount of 5% on this order.

□ご要望にお応えして、5%値引きさせていただきます。
In reply to your request, we would like to reduce the price by 5%.

**カウンターオファーを条件付きで承諾する**

□一度に30個以上のご注文をいただけるようでしたら、10%の特別値引きをいたします。
We can prepare to offer you a special discount of 10% on condition that you place an order for 30 or more at one time.

□一括でお支払いいただければ、20%の特別値引きをいたします。
We will give you a special discount of 20% if you pay all at once.

□これは、通常の値引きとは異なります。

This offer is not subject to the usual discount.

□2～3日考える時間をいただけませんか。

Could you give us a couple of days to think it over?

# ⑤交渉に対する断り

交渉内容を受諾できず、商談成立にほど遠い場合でも、今後のビジネスのことを考慮して丁重に断りましょう。

---

Subject: Re: Request for discount

Dear Mr. Jones:

We have received your counteroffer of July 28th requesting a reduction in price.
We are sorry, but we cannot offer a 20% discount.
However, a 15% discount is available for an order of more than 800.

We look forward to hearing from you again.

Sincerely,

---

件名：Re:値引きのお願い

ジョーンズ様

7月28日付けの、値引き依頼のカウンターオファーを受領いたしました。
申し訳ございませんが、20%の値引きにはお応えできません。
しかし、800個より多くご注文をいただければ、15%値引きさせていただきます。

お返事をお待ちしております。

---

51

| □~%値引きする | reduce the price by ~% |
|---|---|
| □~%値引きする | discount the price by ~% |
| □~%の値引き | reduction of ~% |
| □~%の値引き | discount of ~% |

## Useful Expressions
## 応用表現

**カウンターオファーに対する返事**

□貴社のカウンターオファーには応じられません。
We cannot accept your counteroffer.

□貴社のご提案を検討しましたが、要求を満たせないという結論になりました。
We have considered your proposal, and we have decided that we can't meet your requirements.

□申し訳ございませんが、1台につき400ドルという値段での貴社の注文には応じられません。
We regret that we are unable to accept your order at the price of $400 per unit.

□これ以上の値引きには応じられません。
We cannot offer a further discount.

□これ以上の値引きには応じられません。
We cannot offer an additional reduction in price.

□これ以上の値引きはできません。
We cannot offer a further price reduction.

□それが精一杯の価格です。
I am afraid that is our best price.

□これが提供できる最低価格です。

This is the lowest price we can offer.

□分割払いには応じられません。

We are sorry, but we don't accept payments in installments.

□分割出荷には応じられません。

We are sorry, but we cannot make partial shipments.

□ご要望の納期はお約束できません。

We cannot guarantee the delivery date you require.

### その他・結びの挨拶

□私どもの見積りは、最大限の努力をしたものです。

Our quote is the best effort we can make.

□ご要望にお応えできず、大変申し訳ありません。

We are very sorry that we cannot accept your request.

□弊社の状況をご理解いただきたく存じます。

We hope you will understand our situation.

□他の方法でお手伝いできることがありましたら、ご連絡ください。

Please let us know if we can be of help in other ways.

# 3. 注　文

## ①発注する

商品番号、商品名、型番、数量、色、見積り金額、値引き、出荷方法、納期、支払条件など、必要な条件を書き、注文内容が明確に伝わるようにしましょう。

---

Subject: Order for your dishes

Dear Ms. Smith:

We would like to order as follows:
－300 flower dishes
－100 animal dishes

We haven't confirmed the payment terms.
Is it possible to pay in installments?
Please e-mail us about the payment terms.

Thank you in advance.

---

件名：皿の注文

スミス様

次の通り注文いたします。
・花柄の皿300枚
・動物柄の皿100枚

支払条件を確認していませんでした。
分割払いは可能ですか？
支払条件をEメールでご連絡ください。

よろしくお願いいたします。

## Words and Phrases

| | |
|---|---|
| □注文、注文する | order |
| □注文する | place an order |
| □購入する | buy／purchase |
| □注文書 | purchase order（sheet）／order sheet |
| □急ぎの注文 | rush order |
| □取引条件 | terms and conditions |
| □納期 | delivery date |
| □納品予定日 | expected delivery date |
| □カタログの〜ページにある | on page 〜 of your catalog |
| □引き渡し条件 | delivery terms |
| □支払条件 | payment terms |
| □注文番号 | （purchase）order number |

## Useful Expressions
### 応用表現

#### 見積り、オファーの御礼を述べる

□お見積りをお送りいただきまして、ありがとうございました。
Thank you for sending your price quote.

□11月15日付けのオファーをありがとうございました。
Thank you for your offer of November 15th.

□お見積り条件を承諾いたします。
We accept the terms of your price quote.

#### 発注する

□下記の通り注文いたします。
We would like to order as follows:

□次の取引条件により発注いたします。

We would like to place an order with the following terms and conditions.

□コンピュータ3台を注文させていただきます。

We would like to order three computers.

□次の商品を3個ずつ注文いたします。

We would like to order three of each of the following items:

□カタログの150ページにある机を9台注文したいのですが。

We would like to order nine desks listed on page 150 of your catalog.

□DS-W型のノート型コンピュータを20台注文することにしました。

We decided to place an order 20 DS-W laptop computers.

□A-1型とA-2型のプリンタを2台ずつ注文したいのですが。

We would like to order two units each of the A-1 and the A-2 printers.

□バッグを卸売りしていただけますか。

Can you offer the bags wholesale?

□注文書を添付します。

Attached is our purchase order sheet.

□PDF形式の注文書を添付いたします。

Attached is our order sheet in PDF format.

□1台600ドルのプリンタ10台の注文書をお送りします。

We will send you our order form for 10 printers at $600 per unit.

□これは急ぎの注文です。

This is a rush order.


### 納期に関して

□品物は9月5日までに納品していただくようお願い申し上げます。

We would remind you that the products must be delivered before September 5th.

□2週間以内に発送していただければ幸いです。

We would appreciate shipment within two weeks.

□1月号のカタログに掲載したいので、注文の商品を12月中旬までに受領することはできますか。

Would it be possible to receive my order by the middle of December as we have listed this product in our January catalog?

□納期をお知らせください。

Please let us know the delivery date.

□いつ出荷していただけますか。

When can you ship the goods?

## 支払いに関して

□支払方法を知りたいのですが。

We would like to know the method of payment.

□注文のお支払いをどうすればいいか教えてください。

Please let us know how we can pay for the order.

□クレジットカード以外の支払方法はありますか。

Are there any other ways to pay apart from a credit card?

□Eメールで支払条件をご連絡ください。

Please let me know the payment terms by e-mail.

## 価格について確認する

□単価を確認させていただきたいのです。

We would like to confirm the unit price.

□合計金額が500米ドルだということを確認したいのです。

We would like to confirm that the total amount would be US$500.

□合計金額は500米ドルでよろしいですか。

The total amount would be US$500. Is that correct?

□見積り価格を確認させていただきたいので、前にいただいたメールを添付いた
します。

I attach your last e-mail because I would like to confirm the price you
quoted.

## その他・質問・確認

□卸売り価格にしていただく最低注文数はいくつですか。

What is the minimum order for a wholesale price?

□この手配が大丈夫かどうか、ご連絡ください。

Please let us know if this arrangement is suitable.

□取引条件をご確認ください。

Please confirm the terms and conditions.

□注文を確認してください。

Please confirm this order.

□追加注文で、F98-V3を3つ注文したいのですが。

We would like to place an additional order, three of F98-V3.

□品物を返品することは可能ですか。返品規約はありますか。

Is it possible to return the goods? Do you have a return policy?

□返品規約の有効期間はどのくらいですか。

How long is your return policy good for?

## ②注文内容の確認

受注後、注文内容を確認するメールを出します。その中で、出荷予定、納期などについて述べます。

---

Subject: order confirmation

Dear Mr. Jones:

Thank you for your order dated July 2nd for 300 flower dishes and 100 animal dishes.
Your confirmation number is 01-2105.
We will ship them tomorrow.

We look forward to your order again soon.

Sincerely,

---

件名：ご注文の確認

ジョーンズ様

7月2日に、花の皿300枚と動物の皿100枚をご注文いただきありがとうございました。
貴社の確認番号は、01-2105です。
明日品物を出荷いたします。

またのご注文をお待ちしております。

---

| | |
|---|---|
| □注文番号 | order No.／P.O. No. |
| □注文請書 | order acknowledgement |
| □確認する | confirm／make sure |
| □認める、受領を知らせる | acknowledge |
| □確認番号 | confirmation No. |
| □出荷日 | shipping date |
| □納品日 | delivery date |
| □ご要望どおり | As requested／per your request |

## Useful Expressions
### 応用表現

注文の御礼を述べる

□ご注文ありがとうございます。
Thank you for your order.

□ご注文いただき、光栄です。
We are pleased to have received your order.

□初のご注文に感謝いたします。
We appreciate your first order.

□お取引に感謝いたします。
We appreciate your business.

□ガーデニングの本5冊をご注文いただき、ありがとうございます。
We appreciate your order for five gardening books.

## 注文内容を確認する

□ご注文を確認させてください。

Let me confirm your order.

□貴社の注文を次のとおり確認させていただきます。

We confirm your order as follows:

□これは、7月10日付けのコンピュータ20台のご注文を確認させていただくものです。

This is to confirm your order dated July 10th for 20 computers.

□プリンタ100台の受注を確認させていただきたく、本メールをお送りしています。

This e-mail was sent to acknowledge receipt of your order for 100 printers.

□ご注文の商品番号を確認させていただくため、メールを差し上げております。

I am writing to confirm your order item number.

□注文確認書を添付いたします。

We are attaching the order confirmation.

□貴社の確認番号は、C1234です。

Your confirmation No. is C1234.

□お支払方法を伺いたいのです。

We would like to know the method of payment.

## 納期を知らせる

□ご注文の品は8月10日までにお届けします。

We will deliver your order by August 10th.

□確定した納品日はお知らせできません。

We are unable to give you a firm date for delivery.

□出荷部門より、出荷日について事前にお知らせいたします。

Our Shipping Department will notify you of the shipping date in advance.

□すぐに発送させていただきます。
We will ship them right away.

□ご注文の品は在庫がございますので、すぐに発送させていただきます。
As we have your order in stock, we will be able to ship right away.

□1ヶ月以内にご注文の品をお届けします。
You should receive your order in a month.

## その他・結びの挨拶

□必ずこの新モデルに満足していただけることと存じます。
We are sure you will be pleased with this new model.

□ご質問がございましたら、お知らせください。
Please let us know if you have any questions.

□お取引いただき、ありがとうございます。
Thank you for your business.

□また貴社とお取引させていただけることを楽しみにしています。
We look forward to working with you again .

□また近日中にご奉仕させていただくことを楽しみにしています。
We look forward to serving you again soon.

□本注文が末永いお付き合いにつながれば幸いです。
We hope this order will lead to a long relationship with us.

# ③注文・交渉に応じられない旨を伝える

注文に応じられない場合でも、問い合わせや注文に対する感謝の意を表します。
そして、注文に応じられない理由、代替品の提案などについて述べます。

Subject: The A2000 computer

Dear Mr. Jones:

Thank you for your inquiry of the A2000 computer.
We are sorry that we no longer manufacture that product.
However, we offer upgrade products such as the A3000 or the A3500.
You can see the information on the products at our web site:
http://www.abc.com

If you need additional information, please do not hesitate to contact us.

Sincerely,

---

件名：A2000型コンピュータ

ジョーンズ様

A2000型コンピュータに関するお問い合わせをいただき、ありがとうございました。
申し訳ございませんが、その製品はすでに製造を中止しております。
しかし、A3000型やA3500型のようなアップグレード製品を提供させていただいております。
これらの製品に関する情報を私どものウェブサイトhttp://www.abc.comにてご覧いただけます。

他に情報がご必要でしたら、ご遠慮なくお問い合わせください。

## Words and Phrases

| | |
|---|---|
| □類似品 | similar product |
| □ご参考のため | for your reference |
| □売り切れている | be sold out |
| □在庫がない | be out of stock |
| □在庫がある | have ～ in stock |
| □もはや～ない | no longer ～ |

## Useful Expressions
### 応用表現

**注文の御礼を述べる**

□ご注文いただき、ありがとうございます。
Thank you for your order.

**注文・交渉に応じられない旨を伝える**

□ご注文いただきました製品は、在庫を切らしております。
The product you ordered is currently out of stock.

□ご注文の型はもうなく、新しい型になっています
The model you ordered is no longer available, but the upgraded model is.

□その製品は、型が変更になっています。
The product model has been changed.

□ご注文いただいた製品の新モデルを提供させていただいております。
We offer a new model of the product you ordered.

□ただいま、類似品のA-3型でしたらご提供できるのですが。
We offer a similar product, A-3, at the moment.

# ④注文を変更する／取り消す

注文を変更したり、取り消す場合は、その理由を明確に述べます。

---

Subject: Change of my order

Dear Ms. Smith:

Thank you for your e-mail.
In that case, we would like to change our order(order No.1234).
Please change from "AB01" to "AB02" and the order quantity to 50.
We would like to confirm our order as follows:

| Item | Quantity |
|------|----------|
| AB02 | 50 |
| AB03 | 50 |

Please proceed with our order.
Thank you.

---

件名：注文の変更

スミス様

Eメールをいただき、ありがとうございました。
そのような状況であれば、注文（注文番号1234）を変更したいと思います。
「AB01」から「AB02」に変更し、数量は50個でお願いします。

注文を次のとおり確認させていただきます。

| 品名 | 数量 |
|------|------|
| AB02 | 50 |
| AB03 | 50 |

注文を進めてください。
よろしくお願いいたします。

## Words and Phrases

| | |
|---|---|
| □取り消す | cancel |
| □変更する | change |
| □〜のため | due to 〜 |
| □納期遅延 | delay of delivery |

## Useful Expressions
### 応用表現

#### 注文を変更する

□9月20日に注文したものの数量を変更したいのです。

We would like to change the quantity of our order that we placed on September 20th.

□昨日注文しましたシャツの色を変更したいのです。

We would like to change the color of the shirts that we ordered yesterday.

□白から青に変更してくださるよう、お願いいたします。

We request the color to be changed from white to blue.

#### 注文を取り消す

□残念ながら、納期の遅延のため、注文を取り消さざるを得なくなりました。

We are very sorry to inform you that we have to cancel our order due to the delay in delivery.

□7月2日までに品物が届かない場合、注文を取り消さなければなりません。

We have to cancel our order if the products have not arrived by July 2nd.

＊注文の取り消し理由がクレームの場合は、7. 苦情・クレームを参照してください。

66

# 4．出荷・発送通知

商品を出荷する（した）旨と、到着予定などを簡単に知らせます。

---

Subject: Shipment of your order

Dear Mr. Latry:

The products you ordered were shipped on September 18th, 2003
and is scheduled to arrive in New York on September 20th, 2003.
If you have any questions regarding shipping, please e-mail our
Shipping Department at shipping@abc.com

Thank you for your order.

---

件名：ご注文品の出荷

ラトリー様

ご注文の商品を2003年9月18日に出荷いたしました。
積送品は、ニューヨークに2003年9月20日に到着する予定です。
出荷についてのご質問は、我々の出荷部門であるshipping@abc.com
までEメールにてご連絡ください。

ご注文ありがとうございました。

## Words and Phrases

| | |
|---|---|
| □出荷する | ship |
| □到着する | arrive |
| □配達する、引き渡す | deliver |
| □航空便で | by air |
| □船便で | by sea／by surface |
| □到着予定日 | estimated arrival date |
| □船積書類 | shipping document |
| □船荷証券番号 | B／L No. |
| □航空貨物受取証 | air waybill |

## Useful Expressions
### 応用表現

**出荷について述べる**

□2003年8月24日に、注文番号1234を出荷いたしました。
We shipped your order No.1234 on August 24th, 2003.

□ご注文番号1234は、航空便にて出荷されました。
Your order No.1234 has been shipped by air.

□ご注文番号A-800は、今朝、2003年9月6日午前8:30にサンフランシスコに向けて神戸を出港しました。
Your order No. A-800 left Kobe for San Francisco this morning, September 6th, 2003 at 8:30 a.m.

**納品日について述べる**

□到着予定日は、2003年10月27日です。
The estimated arrival date is October 27th, 2003.

□サンフランシスコへの到着予定日は、2003年10月27日です。

The estimated arrival date in San Francisco is October 27th, 2003.

□ご注文の商品は、2003年10月27日頃サンフランシスコに到着する予定です。

The products you ordered are due to arrive in San Francisco on approximately October 27th, 2003.

□ご注文の品は、遅くとも2003年12月10日までに納品いたします。

The order will be delivered no later than December 10th, 2003.

□2003年12月10日までに品物が届かなければご連絡ください。

Please contact us if you do not receive the products by December 10th, 2003.

□当社の商品資料は、2、3日中に届くはずです。

Our product information should arrive in a few days.

□今月終わりにはご注文の品が届くはずです。

You should receive the product you ordered by the end of this month.

## 請求書について

□商品ご到着後、10日間以内にお支払いいただくようお願い申し上げます。

We would like to request payment within 10 days of delivery.

□後日、請求書をお送りします。

We will send you our invoice later.

□請求書を箱の中に同梱いたします。

We will enclose our invoice in the package.

□請求書をご確認ください。

Please confirm our invoice.

□ご注文の品の現況をオンラインでお調べいただけます。

You can check the progress of your order online.

□受領をEメールでお知らせください。

Please confirm your receipt via e-mail.

□品物を受領されたらお知らせください。

Please let us know when you receive the products.

□航空貨物受取証をお送りします。

We will send you the air waybill.

□ご注文ありがとうございました。

Thank you for your order.

□またのご注文をお待ちしています。

We look forward to your order again.

---

【日付の記載順序】

日付の記載順序は、アメリカ式とヨーロッパ式で異なるため、数字だけで記載すると誤解を招きます。月は省略形でもかまいませんが、必ずスペルアウトしましょう。

**アメリカ式**

September 1(st), 2003

**ヨーロッパ式**

 1(st) September 2003

# 5．受領通知

## ①品物の受領

必要に応じ、製品を受領した旨を簡単に知らせます。

また、受領したものに問題がある場合は、その旨を伝えます（「7．苦情・クレーム」参照）。

---

Subject: Confirmation of receipt／Problem

Dear Sir/Madam:

We received three computers on December 5th, 2003.
However, we found that one of them did not work correctly.
Please let us know what to do as soon as possible.

Sincerely,

---

件名：受領確認／問題があります

ご担当者様

2003年12月5日にコンピュータ3台を受領いたしました。
しかしながら、そのうちの1台が正常に作動しません。
どのように対応したらよいか、できるだけ早くお知らせください。

## Words and Phrases

| | |
|---|---|
| □受け取る | receive |
| □配達する | delivery |
| □早急な | prompt |

## Useful Expressions
### 応用表現

**品物の受領を伝える**

□本日、注文の品を受け取りました。

We received our order today.

□取り急ぎ、昨日品物を受領したことをお知らせいたします。

We would just like to inform you that we received the products yesterday.

□新商品の資料をお送りいただきまして、ありがとうございました。

Thank you for your new product information.

□XY-2型コンピュータ5台を早々に出荷していただき、ありがとうございました。

Thank you for your prompt shipment of the five XY-2 computers.

□迅速に納品していただき、ありがとうございました。

Thank you for your prompt delivery.

**欠品について述べる**

□注文番号1234のうち3商品を受け取っていません。

We have not received three products of our order No. 1234.

□2つの商品が入っていませんでした。

Two products are missing.

## 関係書類について述べる

□送り状が同封されていませんでした。

Your invoice was not enclosed.

□航空貨物受取証を受け取っていません。

We have not received the air waybill.

□船積書類をお送りいただきましたか。

Have you sent the shipping documents?

□できるだけ早く、船積書類をお送りください。

Please send us the shipping documents as soon as possible.

海外からは、Eメールだけではなく、ファックスによる問い合わせもあります。ファックスは、文字が薄すぎて読めなかったり、ページが抜けていたりすることがあります。そのようなときによく使うフレーズをまとめてみました。

---

Subject: We received your fax

Dear Mr. Smith:

We received your fax regarding your order of five washing machines.
We will send you your order confirmation by snail mail.

Thank you for your order.

---

件名：ファックスを受領いたしました

スミス様

洗濯機5台の注文に関するファックスを受領いたしました。
普通郵便で注文請書をお送りします。

ご注文ありがとうございました。

# Useful Expressions
## 応用表現

### ファックスの受領を伝える

□ファックスを受領いたしました。
We received your fax.

□昨日、ファックスにて貴社からの注文書を受け取りました。
We received your purchase order sheet by fax yesterday.

### トラブルについて述べる

□受信中に何らかのトラブルがあったようです。
There might have been an error during transmission.

□あいにく、文字が薄くて鮮明でないため、ファックスが読めません。
Unfortunately, we cannot read your fax because the characters were faint and unclear.

□送っていただいたファックスが1ページ抜けていました。
One page is missing from the fax you sent me.

### 再度ファックスを送信してもらう

□5ページのみ、再度ファックスしてください。
Please fax only page 5 again.

□貴社への地図を再度ファックスしていただけませんか。
Could you fax us the map to your office again?

□昨日、何枚ファックスされましたか。

How many pages did you fax yesterday?

□当社のファックス番号は、+81-3-1234-5678です。

Our fax number is +81-3-1234-5678.

□ファックス機に記録されている番号が正しいかどうか、お確かめください。

Please ensure that the fax number recorded in your fax machine is correct.

□XY社より受け取ったファックスを貴社へ転送します。

We are forwarding a fax from XY Corporation to you.

□お手数をおかけして申し訳ございません。

I apologize for any inconvenience.

# ③Eメールの受領

Eメールを受け取ったら、簡単でよいので必ず返信しておきましょう。

機能別Eメールサンプル・表現集

---

Subject: Thank you for your e-mail

Dear Ms. Dion:

We received your e-mail regarding your invoice No. 3081.
We will check the problem you pointed out, and get back to you
as soon as possible.

Thank you.

---

件名：Eメールをありがとうございました

ディオン様

請求書番号3081に関するEメールを受け取りました。
ご指摘いただいた問題をチェックし、できるだけ早くご連絡いたします。

よろしくお願いいたします。

# Useful Expressions
## 応用表現

### Eメールの御礼を述べる

□Eメールをいただき、ありがとうございました。
　Thank you for your e-mail.

□このEメールは、あなたからのオンライン注文を受け付けたことを確認するものです。
　This e-mail is to confirm that we have received your order online.

### トラブル・質問・依頼

□貴社からのEメールを弊社の営業部門へ転送しておきます。
　I will forward your e-mail to our sales department.

□ファックスで送っていただいたデータをEメールで送信していただけませんか。
　Could you e-mail me the data you sent me by fax?

□前回送っていただいたEメールは、文字化けしていました。
　Your last e-mail was unreadable.

□ファイルを添付するのをお忘れのようです。
　You may have forgot to attach a file.

□送られていないファイルがあるようです。
　It seems that some of the files were not sent.

□ファイルを再送していただけますか。
　Could you please resend the file?

□テキスト形式で送ってください。
　Please send a file in text format.

□添付ファイルを開くことができません。
　I cannot open the attached file.

□お送りいただいた添付ファイルを解凍できません。
　I cannot expand the attachment you sent me.

□間違ったアドレスにEメールを送信されています。
　You sent the e-mail to the wrong address.

□MS-Wordをもっていません。
　I don't have MS-Word.

□こちらのコンピュータにMS-Wordがインストールされていません。
　MS-Word isn't installed in my computer.

□お手数をおかけして申し訳ございません。
　I apologize for any inconvenience.

【不在を知らせる自動送信メッセージ】
不在の間に届いたメールに自動的に返信する場合のメッセージ例です。

Thank you for your message.
I'm out of the office until Friday, September 10th.
If your matter is urgent, please call me at 090-1234-5678, otherwise
I'll contact you upon my return.

Best Regards,

Eメールをいただき、ありがとうございます。
9月10日（金）まで不在です。
緊急の場合は、090－1234－5678までお電話ください。お急ぎでなけれ
ば、戻り次第ご連絡いたします。

# 6．支払いの督促

## ①初回の督促

支払いの督促状を初めて出す場合は、相手や銀行の手違いも考えられますので、支払いを促す程度の軽い督促状にとどめておきましょう。

---

Subject: Invoice No. 4718

Dear Accounting Manager:

This is just to remind you that your payment is overdue.
Our invoice No. 4718 for $1,500 has not been paid yet.
Please check your record, and let us know if you have any
questions regarding this payment.

If payment has already been made, please disregard this e-mail.
Thank you.

---

件名：請求書番号4718について

経理部長様

これは、貴社のお支払いが期日を過ぎていることをお知らせするものです。
請求書番号4718の1,500ドルがまだ支払われておりません。
記録をご確認のうえ、このお支払いについてご質問がございましたら
ご連絡ください。

お支払いがお済みでしたら、本メールを無視してください。
よろしくお願いいたします。

## Words and Phrases

| | |
|---|---|
| □支払う | pay |
| □支払い | payment |
| □勘定書、計算書 | account |
| □請求書、送り状 | invoice |
| □請求明細書 | statement |
| □督促状、催促状 | reminder |
| □未払いの | outstanding |
| □未払いの支払い | outstanding payment |
| □支払期日のきた | due |
| □支払いの期日 | due date |
| □期限が過ぎた | overdue |
| □送金する | remit |
| □送金 | remittance |
| □清算する | clear one's account |
| □清算する | settle |
| □私どもの記録によると | according to our records, |

## Useful Expressions

### 応用表現

**未払いについて伝える**

□これは、支払いの期日が過ぎていることをお知らせするものです。

This is just a friendly reminder to inform you that your account is overdue.

□8月15日にご注文いただきましたノート型パソコン（注文番号2382）の代金が支払われておりません。

We would like to remind you of your outstanding payment for the laptop computer ordered on August 15th (order No. 2382).

□弊社の記録によると、請求書No.6489が未払いになっています。

Our records show that invoice No. 6489 is still outstanding.

□350ドルの未払いがあります。

We find that there is an outstanding balance of $350.

## 支払期限について述べる

□本支払いのお支払期限は、9月30日でした。

The due date for this payment was September 30th.

□契約条件によると、お支払いの期限は12月31日でした。

According to the terms of our contract, your payment was due on December 31st.

□お支払いは2ヶ月以内という条件だったと思いますが。

We would like to remind you that our terms were to make payment within two months.

## 支払いを促す

□至急送金していただければ幸いです。

Your prompt remittance will be very much appreciated.

□すぐにお支払いいただけるのをお待ちしております。

We look forward to your prompt payment.

## 連絡をもらう

□できるだけ早くご連絡ください。

Please contact us as soon as possible.

□請求書についてのお問合わせは、03-1234-5678までご連絡ください。

For inquires about your invoice, please call us at 03-1234-5678.

□請求書についてご質問がございましたら、ご連絡ください。

If you have any questions about your invoice, please contact us.

□記録をご確認ください。

Please check your records.

□詳細は添付した明細書のとおりです。

The details are shown on the attached statement.

□もしお支払い済みでしたら、本メールを無視してください。

If you have already settled the amount, please disregard this e-mail.

2回目以降の督促状については、1回目より強く支払いを求める内容にします。

---

Subject: Second reminder

Dear Mr. Latry:

We still have not received your response to the overdue payment despite our e-mail on April 10th.
We would like you to remit immediately or inform us about the reason this payment is delayed.

We wish again to call your immediate attention to your outstanding invoice.

Sincerely,

---

件名：2度目の督促状

ラトリー様

4月10日にEメールをお送りしましたが、いまだに未払いに対するお返事をいただいておりません。
早急にお支払いいただくか、このお支払いが遅れている理由を教えていただきたいのです。

未払いの請求書に対して至急ご配慮していただきますよう、再度お願い申し上げます。

## Words and Phrases

| | |
|---|---|
| □最終通達 | final notice |
| □法的手段 | legal action |
| □回収業者 | collection agency |
| □至急 | immediately |
| □〜までに | no later than 〜 |

## Useful Expressions
### 応用表現

**未払いについて伝える**

□7月10日にご連絡しましたとおり、代金がいまだに支払われておりません。
As we notified you on July 10th, the payment is still overdue.

□このメールは、未払いになっている請求書No.4916に関する3回目のEメールです。
This is the third e-mail we have sent you regarding our invoice No. 4916 which has not been settled.

□次の2つの金額が支払期日を過ぎています。
 ・2003年4月1日付け、請求書No.0001の1,000ドル
 ・2003年5月3日付け、請求書No.0002の2,500ドル
The following two amounts are overdue.
　-Invoice No. 0001 dated April 1st 2003 for $1,000.
　-Invoice No. 0002 dated May 3rd 2003 for $2,500.

**支払期限について述べる**

□お支払期限から3ヶ月が経っています。
Three months from the due date has passed.

□支払期日から5ヶ月以上も過ぎています。

This amount is now more than five months overdue.

□お支払いが2ヶ月遅れています。

Your payment is now two months overdue.

## 支払いを促す

□至急、代金1,000ドルをお支払いいただくようお願い申し上げます。

Please remit payment of $1,000 promptly.

□7月30日までに全額お支払いください。

Please make your payment in full by July 30th.

□3月31日までに必ずお支払いください。

Please pay no later than March 31st.

□できるだけ早くお支払いください。

Please pay as soon as possible.

## 最後通告する

□これが最終通達です。

This is the final request.

□これ以上支払いが遅延されるようであれば、取引を終結せざるを得なくなります。

We have to tell you that any further delay on your payment will terminate our business partnership.

□法的手段を取らざるを得ません。

We will have to take legal action.

□貴社の請求書を回収業者に回さざるを得ません。

We will have to turn your account over to our collection agency.

□お支払いいただけない理由があるのであればお知らせください。

Please inform us if there is a reason why this balance cannot be paid.

□いつお支払いいただけるのかをご連絡ください。

Please inform us when we may expect your payment.

□請求書番号3081のコピーをファックスいたします。

We will fax a copy of our invoice No. 3081.

Ⅱ

機能別Eメールサンプル・表現集

# 7．苦情・クレーム

## ①不良品・品違い・欠品に対する苦情・クレーム

注文番号や発注日などを明確にし、どのような問題があったのか、またその問題にどのように対処してもらいたいのかを述べます。

---

Subject: Damaged items

Dear Sir/Madam:

We received our order (P.O. No. 6489) on July 3rd.
Unfortunately, 20 out of 100 cups were badly damaged.
We can't sell them in such condition, so would like to ask you for a refund of them.
Please also let us know what we should do with the damaged cups.

Your prompt response is appreciated.

Sincerely,

---

件名：破損商品

ご担当者様

注文の品物（注文番号6489）を7月3日に受領いたしました。
残念ながら、カップ100個のうち20個がひどく破損していました。
このような状態のものを売ることはできませんので、破損しているカップの返金をお願いしたいのです。
また、破損しているカップをどうすればよいかお知らせください。

早急にお返事いただければ幸いです。

## Words and Phrases

| | |
|---|---|
| □破損した | damaged |
| □欠陥のある | defective |
| □間違った | wrong |
| □取り替える | replace |
| □取り替え、取り替え品 | replacement |
| □代替品 | alternative |

※replacementとはニュアンスが違う。alternativeは、壊れたものを修理している間に借りる代用品というニュアンスで使う。

| | |
|---|---|
| □残念ながら、～をお知らせします | We are sorry to inform you that ～ |
| □残念ながら、～をお知らせします | We regret to inform you that ～ |
| □貴社の費用で | at your expense／at your cost |
| □返品する | send back |
| □払い戻す、払い戻し金 | refund |

## Useful Expressions
### 応用表現

事情を伝える

**【不良品】**

□不良品でした。

　We found the product to be defective.

□3つのホッチキスが欠陥品であることが分かりました。

　Three staplers have been found defective.

□電子レンジが部分的に破損していました。

　The microwave was partially damaged.

**【品違い】**

□間違った商品が届きました。

　We received the wrong merchandise.

□6月10日に注文したものとは違うものが届きました。

We received the incorrect item for our order of June 10th.

□商品の色が違っています。

The color of the product is incorrect.

□サイズが違います。

The size is wrong.

【欠品】

□デジタルカメラを30台注文しましたが、25台しか届いていません。

We ordered 30 digital cameras, but we received only 25.

□配達された数量が、注文数と違います。

The quantity delivered doesn't correspond with our order.

□注文番号1234に関して、商品が2箱足りません。

Regarding order No. 1234, we are two boxes short.

□青色のものがありません。

The blue one is missing.

【その他】

□製品が弊社の仕様を満たしていないことが分かり、大変失望いたしております。

We are very disappointed to find that the product doesn't meet our specifications.

### 対処方法を聞く

□破損品をどのようにすればよいか、お知らせください。

Please let us know what to do with the damaged merchandise.

□どのような選択肢があるのか、お知らせください。

Please let us know what options are available.

□一番早くていつ不足分が配達されますか。

When is the earliest we can expect to receive the missing items?

## 対応を要求する

### 【再発送】

□注文した商品を至急出荷してください。

Please ship the ordered goods immediately.

□8月13日までに不足商品が届くように、出荷の手配をしていただけますか。

Can you arrange the shipment for the missing items to be delivered by August 13th?

□残りの注文品を10月25日までにいただく必要があります。

We need to receive the rest of our order by October 25th.

□できるだけ早く、残りのカップ&ソーサを出荷してください。

Please ship the remaining cup and saucer as soon as possible.

### 【交換】

□商品を交換してください。

Please replace the goods.

□至急、代替品を送ってください。

Please send us replacements promptly.

### 【返品】

□返品したいのです。

We would like to return the product.

□貴社の費用負担で、破損品を返品いたします。

We are returning the damaged products at your expense.

□欠陥品を貴社の費用で返品せざるを得ません。

We have to return the defective product at your cost.

□欠陥品を返品し、全額返金していただくことになります。

We will have to return the defective product for a full refund.

# ②納期遅れに対する苦情・クレーム

品物に関するクレームと同様、注文番号、発注日を明確にし、まず当初の納品予定日やその予定日からどのくらい遅れているのかを述べ、現況や出荷スケジュール等の回答を求めます。

---

Subject: Our order No. 2345

Dear Sir/Madam:

We have not received our order No. 2345 as of March 20th.
We need the products to supply to our customer by April 5th.
Could you confirm that the products will be delivered by March 28th?

Please let us know the shipment schedule immediately.
Thank you.

---

件名：注文番号2345について

ご担当者様

3月20日現在で、注文番号2345が届いておりません。
顧客に納品するので4月5日までに商品が必要です。
3月28日までに商品が配達されるかどうか確認していただけますか。

至急、出荷予定をお知らせください。
よろしくお願いいたします。

## Words and Phrases

| | |
|---|---|
| □出荷する | ship |
| □配達する | deliver |
| □納期 | date of delivery／delivery date |
| □キャンセルする | cancel |
| □～にもかかわらず | despite ～ |
| □～日現在 | as of ～ |
| □遅らせる、遅延 | delay |

## Useful Expressions
### 応用表現

**納期が遅れていることを伝える**

□まだ注文番号1234の品が届いていません。

We have not received our order No. 1234 yet.

□注文の品は、2月12日に納品されるはずでした。

Our order was supposed to be delivered on February 12th.

□契約上の納期からすでに5日間が経ちます。

It is already five days past the contractual delivery date.

□ABC-1型のノート型コンピュータを注文してから約1ヶ月が経ちましたが、まだ届いていません。

It has been about a month since we ordered the ABC-1 laptop computer, and we have not received it yet.

**対応を要求する**

□注文状況を確認してください。

Please check our order status.

□この件について、できるだけ早く調べてください。

Please look into this matter as soon as possible.

□至急、出荷予定を知りたいのです。

We would like to know the shipment schedule immediately.

□12月20日までに品物が必要です。

We need the products by December 20th.

□注文をキャンセルしてください。

Please cancel our order.

□注文をキャンセルせざるを得ません。

We have to cancel our order.

□12月20日までに品物を受領できなければ、注文を取り消さざるを得ません。

We will have to cancel our order if we have not received the goods by December 20th.

# ③請求に関する苦情・クレーム

請求書に記載されている請求金額が間違っている場合は、間違っている箇所を
詳細に記述します。

---

Subject: Error in invoice No. 0001

Dear Accounting Manager:

We received your invoice No. 0001.
Your statement shows that the unit price is $100, but you offered
$80 per unit in your quotation of May 5th.
Please reissue your invoice and send it to us as soon as possible.

Thank you.

---

件名：請求書番号0001の間違い

経理部長様

請求書番号0001を受け取りました。
請求明細では、単価100ドルとなっていますが、5月5日付けの見積書
では単価80ドルとなっていました。
請求書を再発行し、できるだけ早くお送りください。

よろしくお願いいたします。

## Words and Phrases

| | |
|---|---|
| □請求書、送り状 | invoice |
| □請求金額 | invoiced amount |
| □請求明細書 | statement |
| □見積書 | price quote／quote／quotation |
| □再発行する | reissue |

## Useful Expressions
### 応用表現

**請求金額が間違っている旨を伝える**

□請求金額が間違っています。
The amount of the invoice isn't correct.

□請求書番号0001の合計金額が違っているようです。
The total amount doesn't seem right on invoice No. 0001.

□単価は15ドルのはずです。
The unit price should be $15.

□25%値引きで合意したと思いますが。
I thought we agreed on a 25% discount.

□税金は金額に含まれるということで合意したと思いますが。
I thought we agreed that the tax would be included in the amount.

□10%割引が適用されていません。
A 10% discount was not applied.

## 対応を要求する

□請求書を再発行してください。

Please reissue your invoice.

□契約条件を再度確認してください。

Please reconfirm the terms of the contract.

## その他

□請求書と1月15日付けの見積書のコピーをお送りいたします。

We will send a copy of your invoice and quotation of January 15th.

□支払いをすべて完了しております。

We have made all the payments in full.

# 8. 謝　罪

苦情・クレームを受けた場合は、原因を述べるとともに謝罪し、今後の対応について述べます。

**不良品に対する謝罪**

Subject: Damaged products

Dear Mr. Latry:

Thank you for your e-mail of December 25th.

We are sorry that the product delivered was damaged.
We found that the product was damaged during delivery.
Please return the damaged product to us.
We will reship the product this afternoon.

We apologize for any inconvenience this may have caused you.

Sincerely,

---

件名：破損商品について

ラトリー様

12月25日付けのEメールをいただき、ありがとうございました。

お届けした商品が破損していたようで、申し訳ございませんでした。
配送中に商品が破損したことが分かりました。
破損した商品を返品してください。
本日の午後、商品を再送いたします。

この件につきまして、ご迷惑をおかけしましたことをお詫び申し上げます。

Subject: Delayed shipment

Dear Ms. White:

Thank you for your e-mail of December 25th regarding the delay in shipment.

The products you ordered were out of stock at that time, but we didn't realize the fact since our inventory system was down.
We promise that the delay in shipment will never happen again.

We apologize for any inconvenience this delay may have caused you.

Sincerely,

---

件名：出荷遅延について

ホワイト様

12月25日付けの出荷の遅れに関するEメールをいただき、ありがとうございました。

お客様の注文された商品は、在庫を切らしておりましたが、弊社の在庫管理システムがダウンしていたため、そのことに気づきませんでした。
出荷遅延が二度と起こらないことをお約束いたします。

この遅延によってご迷惑をおかけしましたことをお詫び申し上げます。

Subject: Invoice No. 0215

Dear Ms. White:

Thank you for your e-mail of August 21st regarding your invoice No. 0215.

As you pointed out, the total amount was incorrect.
We will be reissuing our invoice.

We apologize for the inconvenience.

Sincerely,

---

件名：請求書番号0215について

ホワイト様

8月21日付けの、請求書番号0215に関するEメールをいただき、ありがとうございました。

ご指摘どおり、合計金額が間違っていました。
請求書を再発行させていただきます。

ご迷惑をおかけして申し訳ございませんでした

## Words and Phrases

| | |
|---|---|
| □申し訳ございませんが | We are sorry that 〜 |
| □〜をお詫び申し上げます | We apologize for 〜 |
| □お詫び | apology |
| □心からの | sincere |
| □遅延 | delay |
| □迷惑 | inconvenience |

## Useful Expressions
### 応用表現

**苦情・クレームについて述べる**

【不良品・品違い・欠品・品質】

□3月14日付けの欠陥品に関するEメールをいただき、ありがとうございました。

Thank you for your e-mail of March 14th regarding the defective goods.

□弊社製品の品質に満足されていないと伺い、大変残念です。

We deeply regret to hear that you were not satisfied with the quality of our products.

□私どものサービスにご満足いただけなかったと伺い、大変残念です。

We are very sorry to hear that you are not satisfied with our service.

【納期・出荷遅れ】

□9月17日付けの、納期遅れに関するEメールをいただき、ありがとうございました。

Thank you for your e-mail of September 17th regarding the delayed delivery.

□申し訳ございませんが、注文番号0001の納品が1週間遅れます。

We are sorry to inform you that your order No. 0001 will be delayed by a week.

□申し訳ございませんが、N5 DVDプレイヤーは現在、在庫がございません。

We are sorry, but the N5 DVD player is currently out of stock.

## 【請求書】

□請求書の誤りをご指摘いただいたEメールをありがとうございました。

Thank you for your e-mail pointing out the error in our invoice.

□請求書No. 324の誤りに関するEメールをいただきました。

We have received your e-mail regarding the error on our invoice No. 324.

□請求に関する誤りをご指摘いただき、ありがとうございます。

Thank you for bringing our billing error to our attention.

## 状況を説明する

## 【不良品・品違い・欠品・品質】

□原因は調査中です。

We are investigating the cause.

□この問題を調査し、できるだけ早くご回答申し上げます。

We will check over this problem and give you the answer as soon as possible.

□Eメールにてご指摘いただきましたとおり、シャツのサイズが違っていました。

As you pointed out in your e-mail, the size of the shirt was wrong.

□出荷物の中に不良品が混じっていました。

There were some inferior goods in our shipment.

## 【納期・出荷遅れ】

□確かに、4月1日にご注文の品を出荷いたしました。

We are sure that we shipped your order on April 1st.

□確かに品物を4月25日に出荷しており、記録もあります。

We definitely shipped the goods on April 25th, and we have record of it.

□先週発送済みですので、なぜいまだに商品が届いていないのか分かりません。

We are not sure why you have not received the products yet since we completed the shipment last week.

□この遅延は、交通渋滞が原因でした。

The delay was caused by a heavy traffic jam.

□商品はただいま輸送中だと分かりましたので、2〜3日で届くかと思います。

We found that the products were in transit, and should arrive in a few days.

□もう2〜3日お待ちいただけますでしょうか。

Could I ask you to wait for a few more days?

### 対応について述べる

**【不良品・品違い・欠品・品質】**

□今朝、代替品を出荷いたしました。

We shipped the replacements this morning.

□代替品を弊社負担で発送いたします。

We will ship the replacements at our expense.

□破損した花瓶を返送していただけますか。

Could you return the damaged flower vase?

□料金受取人払いで商品を返送していただければ幸いです。

We would appreciate it if you would send back the products C.O.D.

□ファックス機が修理可能かどうか見るために、弊社の者をすぐに伺わせます。

We will send someone immediately to see if the fax machine can be fixed.

**【納期・出荷遅れ】**

□配送会社に確認してみます。

We will check the delivery company.

□1週間以内に注文が必ず届くようにいたします。
 We will make sure that your order will be delivered in a week.

□発送を急ぐよう、最善の努力をいたします。
 We will make every effort to speed up the shipment.

**【請求書】**

□請求書を早急に再発行し、お送りいたします。
 We will be reissuing our invoice and send it right away.

□旧請求書はお取り消しさせていただきました。
 We have canceled the old invoice.

□新しい請求明細書をお送りいたします。
 We will send a new statement.

## 謝罪する

□ご迷惑をおかけしましたことをお詫び申し上げます。
 We apologize for your inconvenience.

□この件につきましてご迷惑をおかけしましたことをお詫び申し上げます。
 We apologize for any inconvenience this may have caused you.

□誤送に対し、心からお詫び申し上げます。
 Please accept our sincere apologies for our wrong shipment.

□大変申し訳ございませんが、ご注文の品物の納品が2〜3日遅れます。
 We are very sorry that your order will be delayed by a few days.

□請求書にミスをしてしまい、申し訳ございません。
 We apologize for the error in our invoice.

□間違った請求書でご迷惑をおかけして申し訳ございません。
 We apologize for the trouble with the wrong invoice.

□このような問題が二度と起こらないよう努力いたします。

We will make every effort to ensure that this problem will not happen again.

□ご理解いただきましてありがとうございます。

Thank you for your understanding.

□本件に対するご忍耐とご協力に感謝いたします。

We thank you for your patience and cooperation in this matter.

### 責任を認められない場合

□いかなる責任も負いかねます。

We cannot take any responsibility.

□20個以上ご注文の場合にのみ、値引きが適用されます。

The discount will be applied only for an order of 20 or more.

□弊社の費用負担では、代替品をお送りできません。

We cannot send the replacement at our cost.

□貴社負担であれば、代替品をご用意させていただきます。

We will make arrangements for the replacements at your cost.

□本契約はCIF条件となっております。

This contract is subject to the CIF conditions.

□本件に関しましては、保険会社にお問い合わせください。

Please contact your insurance company regarding this matter.

# 9. 商品案内

## ①キャンペーンのお知らせ

詳細はインターネットで見てもらうなど、Eメールの受信者のことを考え、必要最低限の内容にまとめましょう。

---

Subject: Our Christmas Campaign!

It is time to start our Christmas campaign 2003!

As we informed you by postcard, our campaign starts on November 15th.
During this campaign, you can receive up to 70% off your orders.
To learn more about this campaign, just visit our web site: http://www.abc.com

We look forward to your order.

---

件名：クリスマスキャンペーン！

クリスマスキャンペーン2003が始まります！

はがきでお知らせしましたように、11月15日からキャンペーンが始まります。
この期間中は、ご注文の金額が最大70％オフになります。
このキャンペーンに関する詳細に関しては、当ウェブサイトをご覧ください。http://www.abc.com

ご注文をお待ちしております。

---

## Words and Phrases

| | |
|---|---|
| □キャンペーン | campaign |
| □特別価格 | special price |
| □販売促進 | sales promotion |

## Useful Expressions
### 応用表現

**キャンペーンについて述べる**

□6月28日から8月31日まで、夏のキャンペーンを実施します。
There will be a summer campaign from June 28th to August 31st.

□7月31日までは10%オフになります。
We can offer a 10% discount on the price until July 31st.

□夏のキャンペーン中は20%オフになります。
We will give you 20% off during the summer campaign.

□この期間は、ご注文金額が最大80%オフになります。
During the time, you can receive up to 80% off your orders.

□無料で1ヶ月間、トランクルームサービスをお試しいただけます。
You can try our trunk room service free for a month.

□IP電話サービスを無料で半年間ご利用いただけます。
We can offer our IP telephone service free for six months.

□母の日のキャンペーンが始まります。
It is time to start a campaign for Mother's Day.

□このキャンペーンは、7月18日の金曜で終了します。
This campaign will end on Friday, July 18th.

□数には限りがあります!!

Supplies are limited!!

□もしご希望でしたら、無料サンプル差し上げます。

You can get a free sample if you request one.

□これらの価格は、ウェブサイトからのご注文に限り、適用されます。

These prices will be applied only on orders from our web site.

# ②新製品・サービスの紹介

新製品やサービスを紹介するときには、特徴など、問い合わせや注文につながるような宣伝文句も加えましょう。

何かを発表するときに、"We are pleased to announce 〜"という表現をよく使いますので、覚えておきましょう。

---

Subject: New Consulting Service "e-14001"

We are pleased to announce the launch of our new consulting service, e-14001.

We have been assisted many organizations in achieving the ISO14001 certification, and now we have developed a new consulting method, which is offered on the Internet.
You can learn the details of our e-14001 on our web site:
http://www.abc.com
We would be pleased to send you additional information upon your request.

If you have any questions, please feel free to contact us at info@abc-frontier.com

Sincerely,

---

件名：新コンサルティングサービス「e-14001」

新しいコンサルティングサービスであるe-14001の開始をお知らせ
いたします。

弊社は、多くの組織に対し、ISO14001の認証を取得するお手伝いを行っ
てまいりました。
そしてこの度、インターネット上でご提供する新しいコンサルティン
グ方式を開発いたしました。
e-14001に関する詳細は、ウェブサイト http://www.abc.comにて
ご覧いただけます。
ご要望がございましたら、追加資料のご送付も喜んで承ります。

ご質問がございましたら、お気軽に info@abc-frontier.com までお
問い合わせください。

## Words and Phrases

| | |
|---|---|
| □喜んで〜する | be pleased to 〜 |
| □発表する | announce |
| □新製品 | new product |
| □新サービス | new service |
| □発売する、始める | launch |
| □発売する | release |
| □ご要望にお応えして | upon your request |

## Useful Expressions
## 応用表現

□ABCミュージック社は、膨大な種類のテクノやトランスの音楽ファイルをご提供する新しいウェブサイトを開設しました。

ABC music company has just opened a new web site to offer a vast selection of techno and trance music files.

□新しいダウンロードサービスについての詳細情報は、弊社ウェブサイト http://www.abc.comにてご覧いただけます。

You can get further details of our new download service from our web site: http://www.abc.com

□新製品FW-D3のセールスポイントは、他のどの競合他社の製品よりも小さくて軽いボディです。

The sales point of our new product, FW-D3, is its smaller and lighter body than that of any of our competitors.

□新しいコンサルティングサービスには絶対の自信があります。

We are extremely proud of our new consulting service.

□ショールームのお近くにお越しの際は、ぜひお立ち寄りのうえ、我々の新製品をご覧ください。

Stop by and check out our new products when you come by our showroom.

□ご希望であれば、新商品の資料を喜んでお送りします。

We would be pleased to send you some information on our new product upon your request.

□サンプルをご希望の方は、お知らせください。

If you would like to have a sample, please let us know.

□貴社のニーズを満たすばかりか、ご期待を越えられると確信しています。

We are sure to meet your needs, or even exceed your expectations.

# ③セミナー開催のお知らせ

セミナーの開催の告知は、企業アピールにもなります。セミナーの詳細内容
（日時、場所等）や問い合わせ先などを伝えます。

---

Subject: Our seminar "The Future of the Advertising Business"

We will be holding a seminar "The Future of the Advertising Business."
This seminar is for Japanese advertising agencies.
We will explain future changes in the advertising business, and advise how you should prepare for these changes.

　Date : July 15th, Tuesday
　Time : From 1:00 p.m. to 4:30 p.m.
　Place: Hall A in Shinjuku Center

We encourage your participation.

Please click here if you want to be removed from our mailing list for future seminars.
Thank you.

---

件名：「広告業界の未来」セミナーについて

「広告業界の未来」と題しまして、セミナーを開催いたします。
このセミナーは、日本の広告代理店を対象としています。
広告業界における将来の変化をご説明し、その変化に対してどのよう
に備えるべきかをアドバイスいたします。

　日程：7月15日（火）
　時間：午後1時〜午後4時30分まで
　場所：新宿センター　Aホール

皆様のご参加をお待ちしております。

今後セミナーに関する情報が不要な方は、ここをクリックしてください。
よろしくお願いいたします。

## Words and Phrases

| | |
|---|---|
| □セミナー | seminar |
| □開催する | hold |
| □出席する | attend |
| □応募する | apply |
| □参加する | join |

## Useful Expressions
### 応用表現

**セミナー内容について述べる**

□このセミナーは、外資系企業のマーケティング担当管理者を対象としたものです。
This seminar will target senior marketing leaders from foreign
affiliated companies.

□本セミナーの目的は、11月14日に発売になる我々の新商品の紹介と説明です。

The purpose of this seminar is to introduce and explain our new product, which will be on sale on November 14th.

□このセミナーにて、我々の新しい「顧客データ管理システム」を発表することをお知らせさせていただきます。

We would like to let you know that our new "Client Database Management System" will be presented at this seminar.

## その他

□少なくとも月1回は「企業の社会的責任」についてのセミナーを開催しております。

We hold a seminar on "Corporate Social Responsibility" at least once a month.

□参加費用はお一人様8,000円です。

The price per participant is ¥8,000.

□ご要望により、地図をお送りいたします。

A map is available upon your request.

□このセミナーにご出席いただければ幸いです。

We hope that you will be able to attend this seminar.

□あなたの参加をお待ちしています。

We encourage your participation.

□今回のセミナーについてさらに知りたい方は、お気軽にお問い合わせください。

To learn more about this seminar, please feel free to contact us.

□ 今後のセミナーに関するメーリングリストから削除してほしい方は、Eメールをお送りください。

Please e-mail us if you want to be removed from our mailing list for future seminars.

# 10. 申請と許可

## ①一般的な申請・許可

申請メールには、申請内容とその理由などを記載します。また、申請を許可する場合はその条件などを、許可しない場合はその理由なども記載します。

**申　請**

---

Subject: Request for your permission

Dear Mr. Latry:

This is to ask for your permission to use the data in your book, "You Can Be Happy," for our newsletter.
We would like to reprint the result of the questionnaire about marriage on page 17 of the book.
We will, of course, include the author's name and the book title.
If you would like to include other information, please let us know.

Approval of this request would be greatly appreciated.
I look forward to your reply.

Sincerely,

---

件名：許可依頼

ラトリー様

これは、あなたの「幸せになれるよ」という本にあるデータの使用許可
を求めるものです。
本書の17ページにある、結婚についてのアンケート結果を転載した
いのです。
もちろん、著者名と書籍名は記載します。
他に記載してほしい情報があれば、ご連絡ください。

この依頼を許可いただけましたら幸いです。
お返事をお待ちしております。

## 許可する

Subject: Re: Request for your permission

Dear Mr. Parker:

Thank you for your request to use the data in my book.
I am pleased to grant you the rights to use the data.
Please include my name and the book title.
Of course, no changes in the data will be allowed.

Thank you.

件名：Re:許可依頼

パーカー様

私の本にあるデータを使用したいというご依頼をいただき、ありがと
うございます。
喜んでデータの使用を許可いたします。
私の名前と書籍名を記載してください。
もちろん、データの変更は認めません。

よろしくお願いいたします。

Subject: Re: Request for your permission

Dear Mr. Parker:

Thank you for your request to use the data in my book.
I'm sorry, but ABC Co., Ltd. owns the copyright for the data.
I think the data is available only for non-commercial use.
For further information, please contact them at 03-1234-5678.

Thank you.

---

件名：Re:許可依頼

パーカー様

私の本にあるデータを使用したいというご依頼をいただき、ありがとうございます。
申し訳ありませんが、ABC社がそのデータの著作権を所有しています。
データは、非営利目的にのみ使用可能だと思います。
詳細は、03－1234－5678にお問い合わせください。

よろしくお願いいたします。

## Words and Phrases

| | |
|---|---|
| □申請する | apply |
| □申請 | application |
| □申請書類 | application form |
| □許可する | permit |
| □許可 | permission |
| □許可文 | permission line |
| □転載する | reprint |
| □認める、許可を与える | grant |
| □〜という条件で | on the condition that 〜 |
| □利用できる、役立てられる | available |
| □クレジットライン | credit line |
| □著作権 | copyright |
| □引用する | quote |
| □引用 | quotation |

## Useful Expressions
### 応用表現

申請する

□貴社の新サービスを申し込みたいのです。

We would like to apply for your new service.

□弊社のウェブサイトに、あなたの記事の一部を引用させていただきたいのです。

We would like to quote a part of your article on our web site.

□貴社の新製品についての記事を転載することは可能でしょうか。

Is it possible to reprint the article about your new product?

□貴社のウェブサイトの「採用」ページにあるビジネスマンの画像を、弊社のウェブサイトで使用したいのですが。

We would like to use your picture of a businessman, which is on your recruiting page, on our web site.

□添付ファイルは、私の本の目次とアウトラインです。

Attached file is the table of contents and the outline of my book.

□この依頼を許可いただけましたら幸いです。

Approval of this request would be greatly appreciated.

## 条件について述べる

□他に記載すべき情報があれば教えてください。

If you would like to include other information, please let us know.

□本にどのような情報を記載すればよろしいですか。

What information should I include in my book?

□通常の転載の価格を教えてください。

Please let us know the price of your regular reprint fee.

□著者の名前を記載することを約束いたします。

We promise to include the author's name.

## 申請書類

□必要な資料をお送りいただければ幸いです。

We would appreciate it if you could send us any necessary information.

□必要な申請書類をすべてお送りいただけますか。

May we ask you to send us all the application forms?

## 許可する

□貴社のウェブサイトにだけ使用するという条件で、これらの写真ファイルの使用を許可します。

You have our permission to use these photo files on condition that you use them only for your web site.

□今回一度限りの使用となります。

The usage will be limited for this time.

□必ず次のクレジットラインを印刷してください。

Please make sure to print the following credit line:

□次の許可文を掲載してください。

Please include the following permission line:

□貴社の出版物をお送りいただけますか。

Could you forward your publication?

## 許可しない

□弊社は、すでにいくつかのコンサルティング会社と提携しております。

We are already working with some ISO consulting companies.

□著者が記事の転載を許可しておりません。

The author does not allow the copy of the article.

□その本の著作権は、私にはありません。

I don't have the copyright for the book.

□その本の著作権は、依然ABC社にあります。

The copyright for the book still rests with ABC Corporation.

□当社の教材は、非営利団体に対してのみ利用可能です。

Our materials are available only for non-profit organizations.

□写真の変更やデフォルメは認められません。

No changes or deformation of the picture will be allowed.

# ②ホームページへのリンクについての申請・許可

他社（人）のホームページへのリンクを貼らせてもらいたい、または自分のホームページへのリンクを貼ってもらいたい場合の表現です。

## 申 請

Subject: Request for the link

Dear Sir/Madam:

We are one of the most successful consulting companies in Tokyo.

We visited your web site and would like to make a link from our site to yours.
We also would like to request that our web site be posted on the management consultant index list.
Our URL is: http://www.abc.com

If you have any questions, please contact me at takahashi@abc.com

Sincerely,

---

件名：リンクの依頼

ご担当者様

弊社は、東京で最も成功しているコンサルティング会社のひとつです。

貴社のウェブサイトを拝見し、弊社サイトから貴社サイトにリンクを貼らせていただけないかと考えております。
また、経営コンサルタントのインデックスリストに掲載していただきたいのです。
弊社のURLは、http://www.abc.comです。

ご質問がございましたら、takahashi@abc.comまでご連絡ください。

## ◇注文書◇

| 書名 | 定価 | 円 | 冊 |
|---|---|---|---|
| 書名 | 定価 | 円 | 冊 |
| 書名 | 定価 | 円 | 冊 |

ご住所　〒

お名前　　　　　　　　☎　　　（　　　）

# 愛読者カード

URL：http://www.beret.co.jp/

お手数ですがこのカードでご意見をお寄せ下さい。貴重な資料として今後の編集の参考にさせていただきます。個々の情報を第三者に提供することはありません。

■本書のタイトル

| ■お名前 | ■年齢 | ■性別 |
|---|---|---|
| ■ご住所 〒　　　　　　　TEL | ■ご職業 | |
| ■Eメールアドレス | | |

●本書についてのご感想をお聞かせ下さい。

●こんな本がほしい、というご意見がありましたらお聞かせ下さい。

●DM等を希望されない方は○をお書き下さい。　　　□

●個人情報は弊社の読者サービス向上のために活用させていただきます。

Subject: Re: Request for the link

Dear Mr. Takahashi:

Thank you for your request for a link to our web site.

Please feel free to establish a link to our site.
However, only Japanese consulting companies can be listed on our management consultant list because we specifically target Japanese companies.

Thank you for your understanding.

Sincerely,

---

件名：Re:リンク依頼

高橋様

弊社のウェブサイトにリンクを貼りたいという依頼をいただき、ありがとうございます。

弊社ウェブサイトへのリンクを貼っていただいて結構です。
しかし、弊社は特に日本企業をターゲットとしているため、日本の経営コンサルティング企業のみ経営コンサルタントリストに掲載しております。

ご理解の程、よろしくお願い申し上げます。

| | |
|---|---|
| □〜にリンクを貼る | make a link to 〜 ／establish a link to 〜 |
| □リンク | link |

## Useful Expressions
## 応用表現

**申請する**

□弊社のウェブサイトから貴社のウェブサイトへのリンクを貼りたいのですが。
We would like to make a link from our web site to yours.

□私どもの要望を受け入れていただければ幸いです。
We would greatly appreciate it if you would approve our request.

**許可する**

□我々のロゴマークと画像資料を使用することを許可します。
You have our permission to use our logo mark and photo materials.

□個人的に使うという条件で、我々のファイルを転送することを許可します。
We will give you our permission to transfer our file on condition that you use it for personal use only.

**許可しない**

□残念ながら、弊社サイトへのリンク貼りの申し出をお断りしなければなりません。
We regretfully have to reject your offer of a link to our site.

□申し訳ないのですが、相互リンクを貼ることに関するご要望はすべてお断りしています。
I'm afraid that I have to reject any requests about making any links to each other.

# 11. アポイントメント

## ①アポイントメントの依頼

アポイントメントをとるときには、希望日時があれば記載します。

---

Subject: Appointment to discuss our new project

Dear Brian:

I would like to make an appointment with you to discuss our new project.
As for me, next Tuesday or Wednesday would be preferable.
Please let me know when it is convenient for you.
I look forward to your reply.

Thank you.

---

件名：新プロジェクトについて話し合うためのアポイントメント

ブライアン様

新プロジェクトについて話し合うために、お目にかかりたいのですが。
こちらとしましては、来週の火曜日か水曜日を希望します。
いつがご都合よろしいかお知らせください。
お返事をお待ちしております。

よろしくお願いいたします。

## Words and Phrases

| | |
|---|---|
| □約束 | appointment |
| □〜と約束する | make an appointment with 〜 |
| □〜に面会する | meet with 〜 |
| □目的 | purpose |
| □〜に関して | regarding 〜 |
| □都合が良い | convenient |
| □会うことができる | available |
| □〜を好む | prefer |

## Useful Expressions
## 応用表現

**用件を述べる**

□3月23日に貴社にお伺いしたいのですが。
  I would like to visit you on March 23rd.

□来週、貴社の新しいオフィスにお伺いしたいのですが。
  I would like to visit your new office next week.

□お時間がございましたら、お目にかかりたいのですが。
  I would like to meet you if you have time.

□明朝9時に菅野氏とお会いできませんか。
  Would it be possible to meet with Mr. Kanno tomorrow morning at 9:00 a.m.?

□今週末、工場を訪問して品質システムをチェックする予定です。
  We are planning to visit your factory to check the quality system this weekend.

□私達の訪問の目的は、プロジェクトAについてもっと詳細に話し合うことです。
  The purpose of our visit is to discuss the project A in more detail.

## 都合を聞く

□いつがご都合よろしいですか。
When would be a good time for you?

□来月のご予定はいかがですか。
What is your schedule like for next month?

□何時がよろしいですか。
What time would be convenient for you?

□来週の火曜日の午後はいかがですか。
How about next Tuesday afternoon?

□何日が一番都合がよろしいかお知らせください。
Please let us know what day will be the best for you.

□この3日がご都合悪いようでしたら、ご連絡ください。
If these three days are not convenient for you, please let us know.

## 都合を伝える

□2月14日の午後か、15日の午前にお会いしたいのですが。
I would like to meet you either on the afternoon of February 14th or on the morning of February 15th.

□4月5日か6日に会合を設定していただけませんか。
Would it be possible to set up a meeting with us on April 5th or 6th?

□私は午前中が良いのですが。
I prefer the morning.

□火曜日ならいつでも結構です。
Any time on Tuesday would be fine with me.

相手が提示してきた日程で都合がつかない場合は、代案をいくつか提示しましょう。

Subject: Re: Appointment to discuss our new project

Dear Tracy:

Thank you for your e-mail.

I would also like to discuss several issues regarding our new project, but unfortunately, I won't be here on the day you suggested.
I will be out of town until next Friday.
Could you suggest an alternative date?
I will be available during the following week.

Thank you.

件名：Re：新プロジェクトについて話し合うためのアポイントメント

トレイシー 様

Eメールをいただき、ありがとうございます。

私も、我々の新プロジェクトに関して話し合いたい事がいくつかあったのですが、残念ながらあなたが提案してくださった日は不在です。
来週の金曜日まで出張なのです。
別の日を提案していただけますか。
再来週であれば大丈夫です。

よろしくお願いいたします。

## Words and Phrases

| | |
|---|---|
| □都合が悪い | inconvenient |
| □先約 | previous appointment |
| □出張中 | out of town |
| □他の | alternative |
| □どちらか、どちらでも | either |
| □申し訳ございませんが | I am afraid |
| □都合をつける | make it |

## Useful Expressions
## 応用表現

### 都合がつく場合

□5月15日であればお目にかかれます。
  I can meet you on May 15th.

□5月15日は大丈夫ですよ。
  May 15th is fine with me.

□9月27日の午後はずっと空いています。
  I am free all afternoon on September 27th.

□来週の月曜日の方が良いです。
  Next Monday would be better for me.

□どちらの日でも結構です。
  Either day is fine with me.

### 都合がつかない場合

□その日は先約があります。
  I have another appointment on that day.

□申し訳ございませんが、今週は時間がとれません。
I'm afraid I don't have time this week.

□来週の方が都合が良いのですが。
Next week would be more convenient.

□申し訳ございませんが、彼は明日はたくさん約束があり、とても忙しいので、お目にかかれません。
I'm afraid he is too busy to meet you due to a lot of appointments tomorrow.

□残念ながら、彼女は今日の午後はふさがっています。
I'm afraid she is tied up this afternoon.

□7月8日の代わりに7月7日ではいかがでしょう。
We suggest July 7th instead of July 8th.

### その他

□8月31日の4時から2〜3時間くらい会うことにしませんか。
Could we see each other for a couple of hours on August 31st at 4:00 p.m.?

□午前11時にオーシャンホテルで会うというのはいかがですか。
How about meeting at the Ocean Hotel at 11:00 a.m.?

□どこでお会いしましょうか。
Where shall we meet?

□お会いするのを楽しみにしています。
I am looking forward to meeting you.

# ③アポイントメントの確認・変更

アポイントメントを変更しなければならなくなったときには、できるだけ早くその旨を伝えましょう。

---

Subject: Request for changing our appointment

Dear Tracy:

I am very sorry that I have to ask you to change our appointment.
Something urgent has come up and I have to take care of it soon.
I will fly to Paris the day after tomorrow and will be back on November 3rd.
I will let you know as soon as I return from Paris.

I apologize for the inconvenience.

---

件名：アポイントメントの変更依頼

トレイシー様

大変申し訳ありませんが、お約束の変更をお願いしなければなりません。
急用ができまして、早急に対応しなければならなくなりました。
明後日パリに発ち、１１月３日に帰国する予定です。
パリから戻り次第、ご連絡いたします。

ご迷惑をおかけして申し訳ございません。

□確認する                          confirm

□延期する                          postpone／put off

□もう一度スケジュールを立て直す        reschedule

□〜に対して謝罪する                 apologize for 〜

□不便、迷惑                        inconvenience

□土壇場で、最後の最後で            at the last minute

## Useful Expressions
## 応用表現

### アポイントメントを確認する

□ミーティングの予定を確認したいのですが。

I would like to confirm our meeting schedule.

□全てのスケジュールは予定していた通りです。

Everything is as originally scheduled.

□私の訪問予定に変更はございません。

There is no change with my visiting schedule.

### アポイントメントを変更する

□申し訳ありませんが、約束の日程を変更していただきたいのです。

I am sorry, but I would like to reschedule my appointment with you.

□大変申し訳ありませんが、個人的事情のため、ミーティングの日程を1月20日
に変更させてください。

I am very sorry, but I have to ask you to change the meeting date to
January 20th due to personal reasons.

□約束を午前11時に変更できませんか。

Is it possible for you to change our appointment to 11:00 a.m.?

□ミーティングを来週のどこかに延期していただけませんか。

Could we postpone our meeting to sometime next week?

□プレゼンテーションは、11月13日の午前10時から午後1時に変更になりました。

The presentation has been changed from 10:00 a.m. to 1:00 p.m. on November 13th.

□約束の時間を変更していただけませんか。

Could we change the time of our appointment?

□変更事項が一つだけあります。

Just one thing has been changed.

謝　る

□ご迷惑おかけして申し訳ありません。

I apologize for the inconvenience.

□土壇場になって約束をキャンセルして、大変申し訳ありません。

I am very sorry to cancel the appointment at the last minute.

# 12. 返事の催促

返事などがもらえない場合は、依頼したメール、ファックス等が届いているのかどうかを確認し、返事がもらえるように促しましょう。

---

Subject: Did you get my e-mail?

Dear Sir/Madam:

I am sending this e-mail to check if you have received my e-mail of February 17th.
I requested a catalog of your new products and your order sheet, but I have not received them yet.
Could you please send them by February 25th?

If there are any problems, please let me know.

Sincerely,

---

件名：Eメールを受け取りましたか

ご担当者様

2月17日付けのメールを受信されたかどうか確認させていただきたく、メールを差し上げました。
貴社の新製品のカタログと注文シートを送っていただくようメールでご依頼申し上げましたが、まだ届いておりません。
2月25日までにお送りいただけますか。

何か問題があるようでしたら、ご連絡ください。

# Useful Expressions

## 応用表現

### 依頼が届いているか確認する

□1月15日付けの私からのメールを受け取りましたか。
Did you receive my e-mail of January 15th?

□1月15日付けのEメールを受け取っていただけたでしょうか。
I wonder if you received my e-mail of January 15th.

□まだお返事をいただいておりません。
We haven't received your reply yet.

□私からのEメールを受信されていないのではないかと思っています。
I am wondering if you didn't receive my e-mail.

□3月3日付けの製品カタログの依頼に関するEメールを受信されていると思うのですが。
We hope you have received our e-mail dated March 3rd requesting your product catalog.

### 依頼した内容とこちらの状況を伝える

□ご訪問の件でEメールを送りました。
I e-mailed you about our visiting.

□6月30日に注文したカタログがまだ届いていません。
We haven't received the catalog ordered on June 30th.

□今月末までに注文書が必要です。
We need your order sheet by the end of this month.

□今月末までに貴社の回答が必要です。
We need your answer by the end of this month.

□25N-SH型ミシン9台の見積書をできるだけ早くいただきたいのです。

We would like a quotation about nine 25N-SH sewing machines as soon as possible.

□最新モデルが記載されたカタログをすぐにいただけることを楽しみにしております。

We look forward to receiving your catalog including the latest model soon.

□今月末までにお返事がいただけることを期待しています。

We expect to be able to receive your reply by the end of this month.

□早いお返事をお待ちしております。

We look forward to your prompt reply.

□お忙しいとは存じますが、一刻も早いお返事をお待ちしております。

I know you are busy, but I would greatly appreciate a prompt reply.

## その他

□そちらの記録を調べていただけないでしょうか。

Could you check your records?

□私のメールがサーバにたまっているのでは、と思うのですが。

I wonder if my e-mail is still pooled in your server.

# 13. お 礼

訪問した後や食事に招かれた後には、お礼のメールを出しましょう。

---

Subject: Thank you very much

Dear Mr. Latry:

Thank you very much for taking the time to show your factory.
I have never seen such a clean factory.
I learned a lot from you, especially from your wonderful quality management system. I think the system works very well and it contributes to the prosperity of your company.

When you come to Japan, please visit our factory.

Sincerely,

---

件名：どうもありがとうございました

ラトリー様

お時間を割いて、貴社の工場を案内していただき、誠にありがとうございました。あのような綺麗な工場は見たことがありません。
大変勉強になりました。特にすばらしい品質管理システムは大変勉強になりました。貴社のシステムはとてもうまく機能していますし、会社の繁栄に貢献していると思います。

日本にいらっしゃった時には、私どもの工場にお越しください。

## Words and Phrases

| | |
|---|---|
| ☐感謝する | appreciate |
| ☐〜していただきありがとうございます | thank you for 〜 |

## Useful Expressions
## 応用表現

### 問い合わせに対するお礼

☐お問い合わせいただき、ありがとうございました。

Thank you for your inquiry.

☐弊社の新商品にご関心をお寄せいただき、ありがとうございます。

Thank you for your interest in our new products.

☐早速お返事いただき、ありがとうございました

Thank you for your prompt reply.

### 注文に対するお礼

☐初めてのご注文、ありがとうございます。

Thank you for your first order.

☐ABCマーケットでのオンラインショッピングをご利用いただき、ありがとうございます。

Thank you for ordering online at ABC Market.

☐お取引いただき、ありがとうございます。

Thank you for your business.

☐お取引に感謝いたします。

We appreciate your business.

## お世話になったことに対するお礼

□ご招待いただきましてありがとうございます。

Thank you for your invitation.

□昨夜はすばらしい夕食を誠にありがとうございました。

Thank you very much for the great dinner last night.

□素晴らしい夕食をご馳走いただきまして、大変ありがとうございました。

Thank you very much for the wonderful dinner.

□ありがとう。今夜はあなたと楽しい時間を過ごしました。

Thank you. I had a lot of fun with you tonight.

□すてきな贈り物をどうもありがとうございました。

Thank you very much for the wonderful gift.

□ロンドン滞在中は、案内していただき、誠にありがとうございました。

It was very kind of you to show me around during my stay in London.

□パリ滞在をとても楽しめました。

I thoroughly enjoyed my stay in Paris.

□ニューヨーク滞在中は、ご親切なおもてなしをいただき、大変感謝しております。

I really appreciate your kind hospitality during my stay in New York.

□お忙しいところ、お時間をいただき、ありがとうございました。

Thank you for taking time out of your busy schedule.

□いつかあなたにお返しができればと思います。

I hope that I may have the opportunity to return your kindness someday.

□スタッフの方に感謝の気持ちをお伝えください。

Please extend my appreciation to your staff.

□あなたのヨーロッパ市場に関するアドバイスは大変役立ちました。
Your advice about the European market was very helpful.

□5月15日付けのEメールをありがとうございました。
Thank you for your e-mail of May 15th.

□ファックスをありがとうございました。
Thank you for your fax.

## 感謝の気持ちを表現する

□いろいろありがとうございました。
Thank you for everything.

□サポートしてくれてありがとうございます。
Thank you for your support.

□ご協力ありがとうございました。
Thank you for your cooperation.

□重ねて御礼申し上げます。
Thank you again.

□ご助力に(前もって)感謝いたします。
Thank you in advance for your help.

□ご協力に感謝いたします。
I appreciate your cooperation.

□ご好意に感謝します。
We appreciate your thoughtfulness.

□どれほど感謝しているのかをお伝えしたいのです。
I would like to let you know how much I appreciate it.

□感謝の気持ちをお伝えしたかったのです。
I just wanted to express my gratitude.

# 14. お知らせ

## ①新会社設立・会社移転・住所変更

会社が移転する際は、移転日、新住所、電話番号などを速やかに知らせましょう。

Subject: We are moving

Dear Customer:

This is to inform you that ABC Corporation is moving on November 15th.
Our new address, phone and fax numbers are as follows:
Address: 1-2-3 Nishi- Shinjuku
　　　　　Shinjuku-ku, Tokyo 123-4567
Phone: +81-3-1234-5678
Fax:　 +81-3-1234-5679

Sincerely,

件名：移転します

お客様各位

ABC会社は、11月15日に移転することをお知らせ申し上げます。
当社の住所、電話番号、ファックス番号は次の通りです。
住所：〒123-4567　東京都新宿区西新宿 1-2-3
電話：+81-3-1234-5678
ファックス：+81-3-1234-5679

## Words and Phrases

| | |
|---|---|
| □～付けで | on ～ |
| □～をもって、～現在で | as of ～ |
| □現住所 | current address |
| □代表番号 | main phone number |
| □内線番号 | extension |
| □直通 | direct |
| □移転する | move |
| □そのままである | remain the same |

## Useful Expressions
### 応用表現

**会社設立のお知らせ**

□2003年9月1日にABC会社を設立いたしましたことをお知らせ申し上げます。

We are pleased to announce that ABC Corporation was established on September 1st, 2003.

□ABC会社は2003年9月1日より業務を開始いたしました。

ABC Corporation has been in operation since September 1st, 2003.

**移転のお知らせ**

□ABC会社は、7月1日付けで赤坂に移転いたします。

As of July 1st, ABC Corporation will be located in Akasaka.

□当事務所は下記の住所に移転します。

Our office will relocate to the following address:

□以下が弊社の新住所です。

The following is our new address:

□町田駅から新しいオフィスへの簡単な地図を添付しました。

Attached is a simple map to our new office from Machida Station.

□5月1日より当社の代表番号が変わります。

Effective from May 1st, our main phone number will be changed.

□5月1日以降の電話番号は次の通りです。

Our phone number after May 1st will be:

□電話番号は変更ありません。

The phone number remains unaffected.

## その他

□お手元の住所録も変更してください。

Please change your records accordingly.

□Eメールのアドレス帳は変更する必要はありません。

You will not have to make any changes to your e-mail address book.

□移転にともない6月30日は休業いたします。

Due to our office moving, we will be closed on June 30th.

□今月末以降は、このEメールアドレスは無効になりますのでご注意ください。

Please note that this e-mail address will be invalid after the end of this month.

□ご不便をおかけして、申し訳ありません。

We are very sorry for the inconvenience.

□こちらにお越しの際は、どうぞお立ち寄りください。

Please drop in when you come this way.

## ②Ｅメールアドレスの変更

Ｅメールアドレスが変更になる場合には、新しいアドレスが有効になる日付や
現アドレスが無効になる日付を明記しましょう。

---

Subject: Change of my e-mail address

To Whom It May Concern:

Since we will change our provider, my e-mail address will be
changed effective April 1st as follows:
takano@abc.co.jp

Thank you.

---

件名：Ｅメールアドレスの変更

関係者各位

プロバイダを変更するため、4月1日よりＥメールアドレスが以下のよ
うに変更になります。
takano@abc.co.jp

よろしくお願いいたします。

## Words and Phrases

| | |
|---|---|
| □有効な | available |
| □ （人）に知らせる | let （人）know |

## Useful Expressions

### 応用表現

□Eメールアドレスが変わりました。
My e-mail address has been changed.

□Eメールアドレスが以下のように変更になりました。
My e-mail address has been changed as follows:

□4月1日よりEメールアドレスが変わります。
My e-mail address will be changed effective April 1st.

□4月1日より私の新しいEメールアドレスは、次のようになります。
Effective from April 1st, my new e-mail address will be:

□転職したため、Eメールアドレスが変更になります。
Since I changed companies, my e-mail address will be changed.

□分かり次第、新しいEメールアドレスをお知らせします。
I will let you know my new e-mail address as soon as I find it.

□このEメールアドレスは、5月31日まで有効です。
This e-mail address is available until May 31st.

□6月1日以降は、このアドレスにメールは送信できません。
You cannot send e-mail to this address after June 1st.

□プロバイダを変えました。
I changed my provider.

## ③出張や休暇に関するお知らせ

長期間不在にするときには、いつからいつまで不在にするのかを述べます。
また、連絡窓口に代理人を立てる場合は、その旨を伝えます。

---

Subject: I'll be away from April 2-9

Dear John:

I am sending this e-mail to let you know that I will be away on business from April 2nd through 9th.
I will be participating in "brush up training" to improve my skills.
I will be back on April 10th.

If you have an urgent matter, please e-mail me at
 <452angel@domoco.ne.jp>, which is the e-mail address of my cellular phone.

Thank you.

---

件名：4月2日～9日まで不在にします

ジョン様

4月2日から9日まで出張のため不在にすることを伝えようと思い、本メールを差し上げました。
スキルアップのために「brush up training」に参加します。
4月10日に戻ります。

何か急用ができましたら、私の携帯メールアドレス
452angel@domoco.ne.jpまでメールを送ってください。

よろしくお願いします。

## Words and Phrases

| | |
|---|---|
| □出張 | business trip |
| □出張する | be out of town |
| □出張のため不在である | away on business |
| □不在の | absent |
| □2週間の不在の | absent for two weeks |
| □不在である | absent／away |
| □産休 | maternity leave |
| □育休 | family leave |
| □産休を取る | take maternity leave |
| □休暇 | vacation |

## Useful Expressions
## 応用表現

### 不在にする旨を伝える

□8月31日の月曜日まで不在です。
I will be out of the office until Monday, August 31st.

□当社は、7月31日から8月5日まで夏休みをいただきます。
We will be closed from July 31st through August 5th for summer vacation.

□9月1日から1年間産休をとります。
I will be on maternity leave for one year from September 1st.

□2月1日に復帰します。
I will be back on February 1st.

□彼女が不在の間、間中次郎が御社を担当いたします。
While I am out, Jiro Manaka will take care of you.

□出張の間は、このアドレスにEメールを送ってください。

　You can e-mail me at this address while traveling.

## 戻ってきてからの対応

□昨日は不在で失礼いたしました。

　I am sorry that I was out yesterday.

□昨夜、出張から戻りました。

　I just got back in town last night.

□産休から復帰しました。

　I am back to work from maternity leave.

□不在の間、問題はございませんでしたか。

　Was everything okay while I was gone?

# 15.　人事異動や退職の挨拶

異動、退職、転職の旨を伝え、これまでお世話になった感謝の意を表します。
また、必要に応じて、今後の予定や連絡先も知らせておきましょう。

---

Subject: I'll be transferred

Dear Mr. Smith:

As of April 1st, I will be transferred to our Yokohama office.
My new position will be Overseas Sales Manager.
Ms. Kana Kimura will take my position.

Thank you very much for your support.
I hope I will have the opportunity to work with you again.

Sincerely,

---

件名：転勤になります

スミス様

4月1日付けで、横浜支社に異動することになりました。
私の新しい職務は海外営業部長です。
木村佳奈が私の後任を務めます。

ご支援いただき、誠にありがとうございました。
また一緒にお仕事をさせていただく機会がございましたら幸いです。

| | |
|---|---|
| □後任となる | succeed one's position／take one's position |
| □〜に転勤になる、異動になる | be transferred to 〜 |
| □〜に出向する | be temporarily transferred to 〜 |
| □〜を担当する | be responsible for 〜 |
| □定年退職する | retire |
| □辞する、辞職する | resign |
| □転職する | change jobs／change companies |
| □支店 | branch |
| □任命する | appoint |
| □子会社 | subsidiary（company） |

## Useful Expressions
### 応用表現

**異動を伝える**

□営業部へ異動になりました。

I have been transferred to work in the Sales Department.

□4月1日付けで、東京本社に転勤になります。

I will be transferred to the Tokyo headquarters on April 1st.

□4月1日付けで2年間、子会社に出向することになりました。

As of April 1st, I will be temporarily transferred to our subsidiary company for two years.

□大阪支店の営業部長に任命されました。

I have been appointed as Sales Manager of our Osaka branch.

## 退職・転職を伝える

□3月31日付けで、ABC社を退職いたしました。
　I have resigned from ABC Co., Ltd. on March 31st.

□3月31日付けで、ABC社を退職することになりました。
　I will be leaving ABC Co., Ltd. on March 31st.

□3月31日付けで、ABC社を定年退職いたします。
　I will be retiring from ABC Co., Ltd. on March 31st.

□4月15日付けでXY社に入社いたします。
　I will join XY Corporation on April 15th.

□転職しました。
　I have changed jobs.

□カフェを始めました。
　I have started a café.

## 後任について述べる

□私の後任者は高橋です。
　My successor will be Mr. Takahashi.

□高橋が後任を務めます。
　Mr. Takahashi will take my position.

□伊藤が貴社を担当いたします。
　Ms. Ito will be responsible for you.

□近日中に彼女から連絡させていただくと思います。
　She will be in touch with you soon.

## 感謝の意を述べる、挨拶する

□ご支援ありがとうございました。
　Thank you for your support.

□これまでご協力いただき、誠にありがとうございました。

Thank you very much for your cooperation in the past.

□貴殿と一緒に仕事をさせていただき、楽しかったです。

I have enjoyed working with you.

□また一緒に仕事をさせていただく機会があれば幸いです。

I hope I will have the opportunity to work with you again.

□貴殿と貴社のご清栄をお祈りいたします。

I wish you and your company all the best.

# 16. 採　　用

## ①採用の問い合わせに対応する

採用に関する問い合わせメールが届いたら、採用内容、条件などを伝えます。
採用を行っていない場合は、その旨を伝えましょう。

---

Subject: Thank you for your application

Dear Mr. White:

Thank you very much for your interest in employment with ABC Corporation.
We require a person who is fluent in English and has good typing skills.

Please send us your career sheet.
After we examine your career sheet very carefully, our hiring manager will contact you by e-mail for an interview.

Sincerely,

---

件名：ご応募いただきありがとうございます

ホワイト様

ABC社での採用に関心をお寄せいただき、誠にありがとうございます。
我々は、英語に堪能で、タイピングスキルをお持ちの方を求めています。

職務経歴書を送ってください。
職務経歴書を詳しく拝見させていただいた後、採用マネージャーより
Eメールにて面接へのご案内をご連絡させていただきます。

## Words and Phrases

| | |
|---|---|
| ☐履歴書 | resume |
| ☐職務経歴書 | career sheet |
| ☐面接 | interview |
| ☐成績、経歴 | record |
| ☐個人情報 | personal data |
| ☐キャリア目標 | career objective |
| ☐技能 | skill |
| ☐資格 | qualification |
| ☐職歴 | work experience |
| ☐学歴 | education |
| ☐経歴 | background |
| ☐応募者 | candidate |
| ☐必要条件 | requirement |

## Useful Expressions
### 応用表現

**問い合わせに対するお礼・挨拶**

☐お問い合わせいただき、ありがとうございます。
　Thank you for your inquiry.

☐ABC社の採用にご関心をお寄せいただき、ありがとうございます。
　Thank you for your interest in employment with ABC Corporation.

☐ABC社にご関心をお寄せいただきありがとうございます。
　Thank you for your interest in ABC Corporation.

☐ブライダルコーディネーター職にご応募いただきましてありがとうございます。
　Thank you for applying for the position of a bridal coordinator.

## 応募条件・ポストについての説明

□現在、翻訳者のみ募集を行っています。
We only have an opening for a translator now.

□堪能なフランス語力が必須です。
Fluency in French is required.

□最低5年は日本に在住していることと、日本語に堪能であることが必須です。
At least five years' living in Japan and fluency in Japanese are a must.

□学生は応募できません。
The candidate can not be a student.

□4年生大学で会計学または財政学の学位と3年超の経験が求められます。
A four-year university degree in accounting or finance and more than three years' experience are required.

□最低でも2～3年の営業経験を必要とします。
The position requires a minimum of 2-3 years of sales experience.

□システムエンジニアのポストについて説明させていただきます。
I will tell you about the position of a system engineer.

□採用された方は、営業マネージャーのアシスタントとして勤務していただきます。
A successful candidate will work as an assistant to the sales manager.

□現在採用を行っておりません。
We are not hiring at this time.

## 履歴書について

□このポストにご興味があれば、履歴書を送ってください。
If you are interested in this position, please send us your resume.

□履歴書をcareer@abc.comまでEメールで送ってください。
Please e-mail your resume to career@abc.com

□日本語と英語の履歴書をＥメールで送ってください。
　Please e-mail both Japanese and English resumes.

## ● 採用の問い合わせサンプル

Subject: Application for Sales Manager

Dear Sir/Madam:

I saw your company's advertisement for the position of sales manager in this morning's edition of ABC newspaper.
I am interested in the position and would like to apply.

I have worked in the Sales Department of AS31 company for two years and I have much experience with the European market.

Thank you.

---

件名：営業マネージャーへの応募

ご担当者様

今朝のABC新聞の朝刊で営業マネージャーを募集との広告を拝見いたしました。
そのポストに興味があり、応募させていただきたく思います。

私はAS31社で2年間、営業に勤務しておりました。
また、ヨーロッパ市場に関して、豊富な経験をもっております。

よろしくお願いいたします。

## ②面接の通知

面接の日時、場所、持参してもらうものなどを伝えます。

Subject: Interview

Dear Mr. White:

I am Michael Brown, chief of the Personnel Department of ABC Company.
Thank you for sending your career sheet.

Would you like to come to our head office in Tokyo for an interview next Wednesday?
Please reply by Friday.

Thank you.

---

件名：面接

ホワイト様

私はABC社の人事部チーフのマイケル・ブラウンと申します。
職務経歴書を送っていただき、ありがとうございました。

来週の水曜日に東京の本社に面接にお越しいただけますか。
金曜日までにお返事をください。

よろしくお願いいたします。

II

機能別Eメールサンプル・表現集

## Words and Phrases

| | |
|---|---|
| □面接 | interview |
| □テスト | test |
| □弊社までの道順 | the way to our office |

## Useful Expressions
## 応用表現

### 面接に関するお知らせ

□明後日10時に面接にお越しいただきたいのですが、可能でしょうか。

We would like you to come in for an interview at 10:00 a.m. the day after tomorrow. Is it possible for you?

□5月10日か5月15日に面接にお越しいただきたいのですが。

We would like you to come in for an interview on May 10th or May 15th.

□簡単な英語のテストを行います。

A simple English test will be given.

□あなたの履歴書を拝見し、お話したいと考えています。

We have reviewed your resume and would like to speak with you.

### 会社までの道のりを案内する

□横浜駅から弊社への道順は次の通りです。

The way from Yokohama Station to our office is as follows :

□小田急線またはJR横浜線の町田駅が、最寄の駅です。

Machida Station on Odakyu line or JR Yokohama Line is the nearest station to our office.

□北口を出てください。
Use the North Exit.

□駅から弊社まで歩いて2、3分です。
It takes a few minutes from the station to our office.

## その他の案内

□面接にお越しになる際に、履歴書をお持ちください。
When you come, please bring your resume.

□ご質問がございましたら、03-1234-5678までお電話ください。
If you have any questions, please call me at 03-1234-5678.

□当社までの地図をファックスいたします。
We will fax you a map to our office.

□履歴書を事前にお送りください。
Please send your resume to us in advance.

□どの職種に興味があるのか、履歴書に明記してください。
Please indicate which position you are interested in on your resume.

□有望者には、面接の前にご連絡さしあげます。
Qualified candidates will be contacted before the interview.

□もしあなたがそのポストにふさわしい能力をお持ちでしたら、採用担当者があなたにご連絡いたします。
If your skills are a match for the position, our hiring manager will contact you.

【会社の地図の英語版】
会社の地図の英語版を用意しておくと大変便利です。

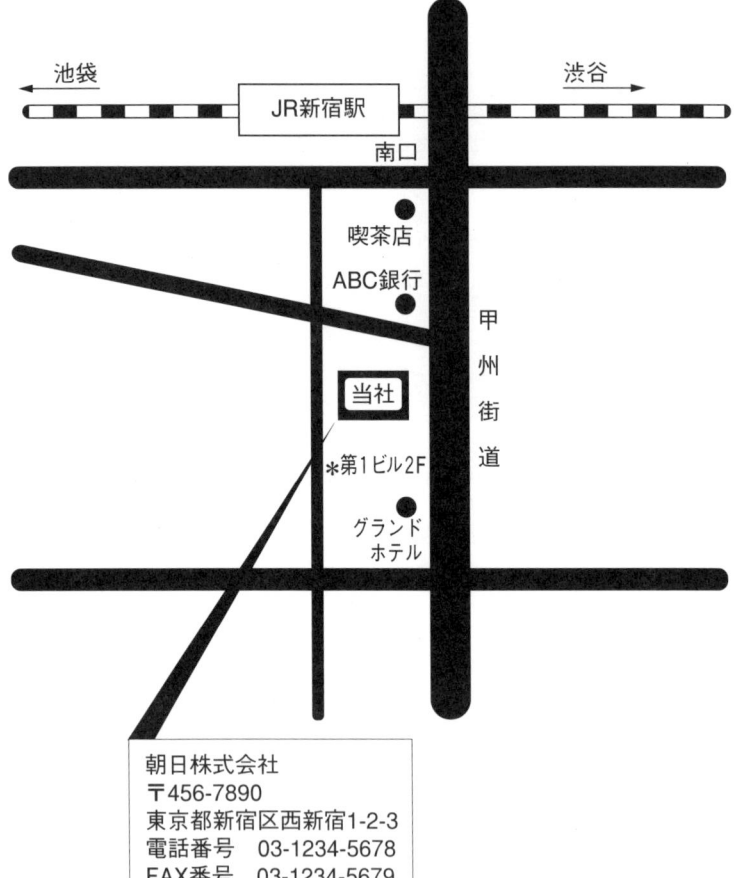

新宿駅南口より徒歩2分

（地図に使える表現）

| 〜駅 | 〜Station |
| --- | --- |
| JR〜駅 | JR〜Station |
| 地下鉄・・・線〜駅 | Subway 〜Station on the ・・・ Line |
| 北（南、東、西）口 | North(South, East, West) Exit |

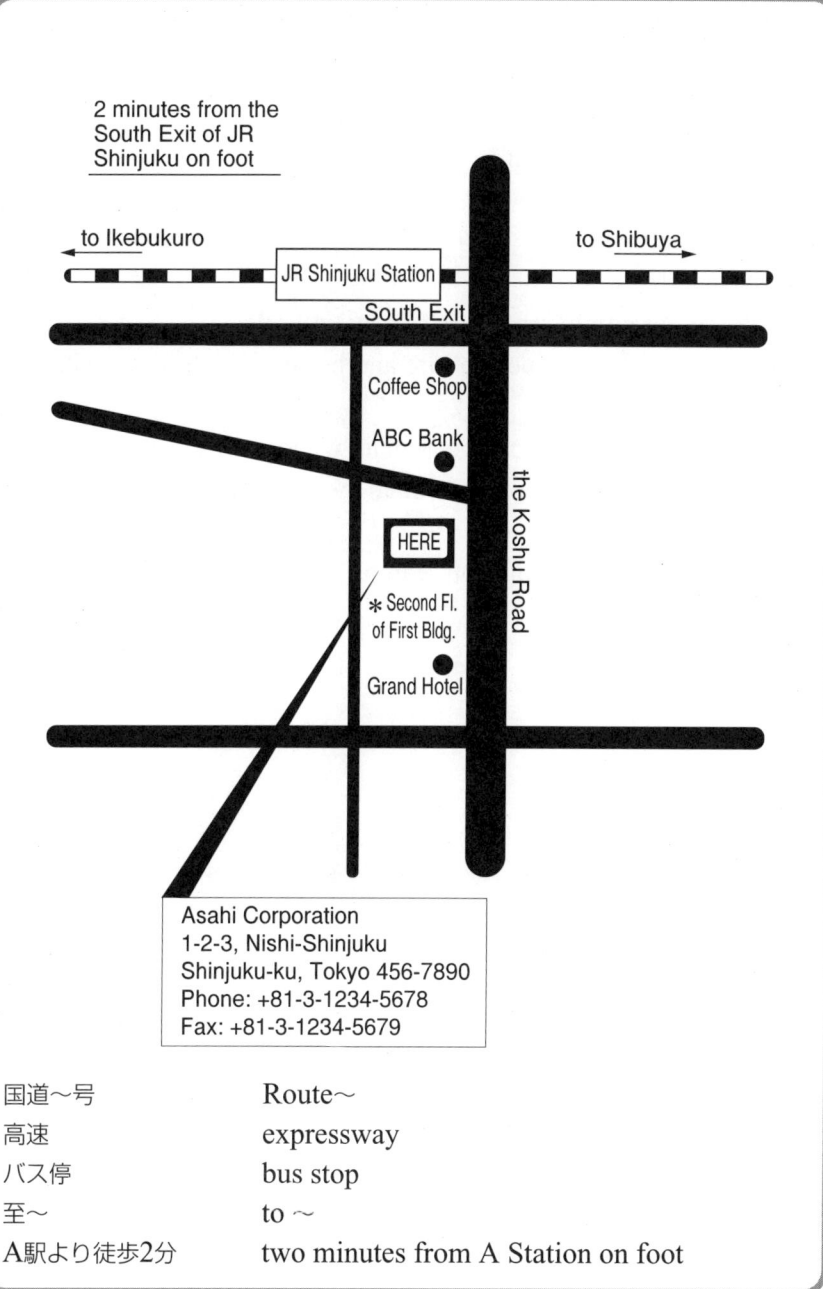

| | |
|---|---|
| 国道〜号 | Route〜 |
| 高速 | expressway |
| バス停 | bus stop |
| 至〜 | to 〜 |
| A駅より徒歩2分 | two minutes from A Station on foot |

# ③採用結果の通知

不採用の場合でも、相手に失礼のない様な文面にしましょう。

Subject: Our employment

Dear Mr. Smith:

Thank you for coming to our interview yesterday.
Unfortunately, we decided to hire another person for the position you applied for.
But, you will be notified via e-mail when a position becomes available that matches your profile in the future.

Best of luck to you in your job search.

Sincerely,

---

件名：採用の件

スミス様

昨日は面接にお越しいただき、ありがとうございました。
残念ながら、あなたが応募なさっていたポストには、他の方を採用することになりました。
しかし、将来経歴に合うようなポストが出てくれば、Eメールにてご連絡させていただきます。

就職活動がうまくいくことをお祈り申し上げます。

## Useful Expressions
## 応用表現

**採　用**

□結果をお待たせして申し訳ありません。

We are sorry to have kept you waiting for the result.

□あなたを英語教師のポストに採用いたします。

We decided to offer you the position of an English teacher.

□営業マネージャーとして、弊社に来ていただきたいと思います。

We would like you to come and join us as a sales manager.

□来月より一緒に勤務できることを嬉しく思います。

It is a great pleasure to work together from next month.

□詳細を話し合う必要があると思います。明日会社へ来ていただけますか。

We need to discuss the details together. Is it possible for you to come to our office tomorrow?

□あなたを採用します。

We have approved your application.

**不採用**

□申し訳ありませんが、営業マネージャーのポストをオファーすることができません。

We are sorry that we are unable to offer you the position of sales manager.

□申し訳ありませんが、このポストにはあなたは不採用となりました。

We are sorry that you are not selected for this position.

□残念ながら、このポストには資格、職歴が我々のニーズに見合う他の応募者を採用することになりました。

Regrettably, we have to inform you that we decided to offer this position to another candidate whose qualifications and work experience meet our needs.

□申し訳ありませんが、あなたの資格ではこのポストには適合しません。

We are sorry, but your qualifications are not suitable for this position.

□あなたのプロフィールに適合する他のポストが空いた際にはお知らせいたします。

You will be notified when there is another position that suits you more closely.

□今後のご成功をお祈り申し上げます。

I wish you every success in the future.

# 17. コミュニケーション

## ①挨　　拶

一般的に、ビジネスEメールでは、直接内容に関係のない時候の挨拶などは省略します。しかし、相手の近況を尋ねたり、こちらの近況を報告するなどして、ビジネス以外の部分で交流を深めていくことも時には必要です。
季節の挨拶については、宗教上の問題もありますので、注意しましょう。

---

Subject: Meeting for our new game software

Dear Lisa:

How are you?

We've just finished developing our new game software!
We're sure the sales will be good.

By the way, I'd like to discuss the advertisement of this software when you have time.
Please let me know when you are available.

Thank you.

---

件名：新しいゲームソフトに関してのミーティング

リサ様

お元気ですか？

こちらはちょうど新しいゲームソフトの開発が終わったところです！
売れると確信しています。

ところで、お時間があるときに、このソフトの広告について話し合い
たいのですが。
いつがご都合よろしいかご連絡ください。

よろしくお願いいたします。

---

【日本の祝祭日】

| | |
|---|---|
| □元旦 | New Year's Day |
| □成人の日 | Coming of Age Day |
| □建国記念日 | National Foundation Day |
| □春分の日 | Vernal Equinox Day |
| □みどりの日 | Green Day |
| □憲法記念日 | Constitution Memorial Day |
| □こどもの日 | Children's Day |
| □海の日 | Marine Day |
| □敬老の日 | Respect for the Aged Day |
| □秋分の日 | Autumn Equinox Day |
| □体育の日 | Sports Day |
| □文化の日 | Culture Day |
| □勤労感謝の日 | Labor Thanksgiving Day |
| □天皇誕生日 | The Emperor's Day |

## Useful Expressions
## 応用表現

**近況を尋ねる**

□お元気ですか。
　How are you?

□最近、どうしていますか。
　How are you doing these days?
　＊"How're you?"よりも"How're you doing?"の方がカジュアルな言い方
　　です。

□どうしていましたか。
　How have you been?

□長い間、連絡がありません。
　I haven't heard from you for a long time.

□どうなっているのですか。
　What's going on?

□相変わらずお忙しいのでしょうね。
　You must be busy as usual.

□仕事の方はいかがでしょうか。
　How's your work?

□景気はどうですか。
　How's your business?

□すべてが順調だと良いのですが。
　I hope everything is OK with you.

□週末はいかがでしたか。
　How was your weekend?

□休暇はいかがでしたか。
How was your holiday?

□休暇の予定はありますか。
Do you have any plans for the vacation?

## 天気・気候について

□今日は暖かく、いい天気です。
It's nice and warm today.

□日に日に暖かくなりますね。
It's getting warmer day by day.

□涼しくなってきました。
It's getting cooler.

□もうすぐ梅雨に入ります。
A rainy season is coming soon.

□ここのところ日本では、とても暑く、蒸し暑いです。
It's been very hot and humid here in Japan.

□ニューヨークでは、ここのところひんやりしています。
It's been chilly these days in New York.

□そちらの天気はいかがですか。
How's the weather over there?

□先週の金曜日から雨続きです。
It's been raining since last Friday.

□昨夜は大雪でした。
We had a heavy snow last night.

□夏は大好きです。
I love summer.

□冬は大嫌いです。
I hate winter.

### 季節の挨拶

□季節のご挨拶を申し上げます。
Season's Greeting!

□新年あけましておめでとうございます。
Happy New Year!

□メリークリスマス！
Merry Christmas!

□良い一年になりますように！
Best wishes for the New Year!

□良い一年になりますように！
May happiness be with you throughout the New Year!

### 仕事について

□新型携帯電話K-10型の売れ行きはいかがですか。
How is your new K-10 cell phone selling?

□クリスマスキャンペーン中の売上げは非常に良かったです。
Sales during the Christmas campaign were really good.

### 結びの挨拶

□働きすぎないように！
Don't work too much!

□お体に気をつけて！
Take care!

□Eメールで連絡を取り合いましょう。

Keep in touch by e-mail.

□鎌倉では、今きれいな紅葉が見られます。

We can see beautiful red leaves now in Kamakura.

□来週、鎌倉に紅葉を見にいきませんか。

How about going to Kamakura to see the red leaves next week?

□いつかあなたを京都へご案内して、日本で一番の季節を体験してもらいたいです。

I'd like to take you to Kyoto someday to experience the best season in Japan.

# ②お祝い（昇進・結婚・出産）

お祝いを伝える"Congratulations on 〜"はどのような場面でも使える便利な表現です。

---

Subject: Congratulations!

Dear Ms. Jones:

I am very delighted to hear that you expanded the business area to Paris.
And congratulations on your appointment as General Manager of the Paris branch office!
I am sure you will succeed in your new position.

Wishing you the very best in your future career.

Sincerely,

---

件名：おめでとうございます！

ジョーンズ様

ビジネスエリアをパリに拡張されると伺い、大変嬉しく思っております。
そして、パリ支店長へのご就任、おめでとうございます！
新しい役職でご活躍なさることでしょう。

将来のご成功を心よりお祈り申し上げます。

## Words and Phrases

| | |
|---|---|
| □ （〜に対して）おめでとうございます | Congratulations on 〜 |
| □昇進 | promotion |
| □任命 | appointment |
| □事業拡大 | expansion of the business |
| □新規事業 | new business |
| □受賞する | win the award |
| □〜ということを聞いて嬉しい | I'm glad／happy to hear that 〜 |

## Useful Expressions
### 応用表現

**会社設立・就任・昇進**

□営業部長へのご就任、おめでとうございます。

Congratulations on your appointment as Sales Manager!

□ご昇任おめでとうございます。

Congratulations on your promotion!

□新会社設立、おめでとうございます。

Congratulations on the establishment of your new company!

□創立50周年、おめでとうございます。

Congratulations on your 50th anniversary!

□横浜支店長として、引き続き新しい地位でのご活躍をお祈りいたします。

We wish you continued success with your new position, as General Manager, Yokohama Branch Office.

## 婚約・結婚・出産

□ご婚約おめでとうございます。
Congratulations on your engagement!

□ご結婚おめでとうございます。
Congratulations on your marriage!

□あなたとジョージが婚約したと聞いてとても嬉しいです。
I am so happy to hear that you and George are engaged.

□あなたがた2人に最高の幸せをお祈り申し上げます。
We wish both of you the best of luck and happiness.

□第1子ご誕生おめでとうございます。
Congratulations on your first baby!

□早く赤ちゃんの写真を拝見したいです。
I can't wait to see the pictures of your new baby!

## その他お祝いの言葉

□心よりご祝福いたします。
Please accept our heartiest congratulations.

□今後のご成功を心からお祈り申し上げます。
Please accept my best wishes for your success in the future.

□お祝い申し上げますとともに、今後のご成功をお祈りいたします。
Please accept our congratulations and best wishes in the future.

□今後もご成功されますようお祈り申し上げます。
Wishing for your continued success.

□お誕生日おめでとうございます！
Happy Birthday!

□お祝いをありがとうございます。

Thank you for your congratulations.

□横浜支店長への昇進に対し、お祝いの言葉をいただきありがとうございました。

Thank you very much for your good wishes on my promotion to General Manager, Yokohama Branch Office.

□婚約に対しまして、お祝いの言葉をいただき、誠にありがとうございます。

It was very kind of you to send us congratulations on our engagement.

□すてきなギフトをどうもありがとうございます。とても気に入りました。

Thank you very much for the wonderful gift! I love it!

□きれいな花をどうもありがとうございました。

Thank you so much for the beautiful flowers!

# ③お見舞い・お悔やみ・励まし

お見舞いやお悔やみなどは手紙で伝えることが多いですが、Eメールで伝える
場合も、あたりさわりのない内容にとどめておきましょう。

### お見舞い

Subject: Get well soon

Dear Suzan:

We are sorry to hear that you are ill.
We all are wishing you a quick recovery.

Best Regards,

---

件名：早くよくなってください

スーザン様

あなたが病気と伺い、お気の毒に思っています。
早期ご回復をお祈り申し上げます。

Subject: Condolences

Dear David:

There are no words to adequately express my deep shock and grief when I heard about the death of your wife.

Please accept my sincere condolences.

Sincerely,

---

件名：お悔やみ

デイビッド様

奥様の死を知らされた時のショックと悲しみは、いかなる言葉でも言い表せません。

心よりお悔やみ申し上げます。

---

## Words and Phrases

| | |
|---|---|
| □心からの | heartfelt |
| □心からの | sincere |
| □弔辞 | condolences |
| □同情・弔慰 | sympathy |
| □深い悲しみ | grief |

176

## Useful Expressions
### 応用表現

**お悔やみ**

□あなたの事故を聞いて、お気の毒に思います。

I am sorry to hear about your accident.

□ブライアンが突然亡くなられたと伺い、ショックを受けています。

We are shocked to hear that Brian has suddenly passed away.

□悲しいニュースを聞いてお気の毒に思います。

I am sorry to hear the sad news.

□ここの皆があなたの事を大変心配しています。

Everyone here is worried about you so much.

□心よりお悔やみ申し上げます。

Please accept our deepest sympathy.

**お見舞い**

□ご病気と伺い、お気の毒に思います。

I am sorry to hear that you have been sick.

□早く回復するといいですね。

I hope you will recover soon.

□早くよくなってくださいね。

Get well soon.

□すぐに仕事に復帰されるよう、お祈り申し上げます。

We hope you will be back to work soon.

□仕事に関しては心配する必要はありません。

You don't need to worry about work.

□昨日あなたのご近所で火事があったと聞いたのですが、ご家族とも大丈夫でしたか。

I heard that there was a fire in your neighborhood yesterday. Were you and your family okay?

## 励まし

□あまり働きすぎないでね！

Don't work too hard!

□元気出してね！

Cheer up!

□何かできることがあれば、お電話ください。

If there is anything I can do, please call me.

## お　礼

□ごていねいにお見舞いをいただきまして、誠にありがとうございます。

I sincerely thank you for your kind inquiries about my health.

□ごていねいにお悔やみの言葉をありがとうございました。

Thank you very much for your kind note of sympathy.

□よくなっていますよ、ありがとうございます。

I'm getting well, thank you.

□だいぶよくなりました。

I feel much better now.

□昨日医者に、あと2〜3日したら出社してもいいと言われました。

My doctor told me yesterday that I would be able to start working in a few days.

□来週の金曜日に退院します。

I will leave the hospital next Friday.

□来週仕事に復帰します。

I will get back to work next week.

# 社内ビジネスメール

## 1. 依　頼

### ①依　頼

仕事を依頼する場合は、具体的な内容や期限などを明確に伝えます。

---

Subject: I'll be out this afternoon

Dear David:

I'll be out to meet with my client this afternoon.
If Mr. Jones of ABC construction Co., Ltd. calls me while I'm out, would you please take a message for me?
Please tell him that I will call him back tomorrow morning.

I don't think that I can make it back to the office today.
Thank you.

---

件名：午後、外出します

デイビッド様

今日の午後は客先に外出します。
もし、外出しているときにABC建設のジョーンズさんから電話があったら、伝言を承っておいてもらえますか。
彼には明日の朝折り返し電話する旨を伝えてください。

今日は会社には戻れないと思います。
よろしくお願いいたします。

II 機能別Eメールサンプル・表現集

179

## Useful Expressions
### 応用表現

□お願いがあるのですが。

Will you do me a favor?

□ネットワークシステムを調べてほしいのです。

I'd like you to check our network system.

□来週の金曜日までにデータがほしいのです。

I'd like the data by next Friday.

□ISO9001に関する情報を探しています。

I'm looking for information on ISO9001.

□見積書を3種類作ってもらいたいのですが。

I'd like you to make three types of quotations.

□倉庫から大きなダンボール箱を5つ持ってきてください。

Please bring five big cardboard boxes from the warehouse.

□社長からのEメールを営業部の全社員に転送してください。

Please transfer the e-mail from our president to all employees of the Sales Department.

□価格表を佐藤さんにファックスしてください。

Please fax our price list to Mr. Sato.

□見積書の日付を7月15日に修正してもらえますか。

Please correct the date of the quote to July 15th.

□あなたの来月のスケジュールを教えてください。

Please let me know your schedule next month.

□今、新しい仕事をあなたに依頼してもいいですか。

Is it possible to give you a new task to do now?

□サーバールームのルーターの調子を見てきてくれませんか。今日はLANが作動していません。

Would you please check the router at the server room? The LAN system doesn't work today.

□打ち合わせの時間を変更してもよろしいですか。

Would you mind if I change the time of our meeting?

## ②依頼に対する対応

依頼内容が不明確な場合は、相手に確認しておきましょう。

---

Subject: I'm attaching the data

Dear Jiro:

I'm attaching the data that you requested.
The file is compressed.
I guess you know how to expand the file.
Please let me know if you don't.
Also, if you have any questions regarding the data, please ask me.

---

件名：データを添付します

次郎様

ご依頼のデータを添付します。
ファイルは圧縮されています。
おそらくファイルの解凍方法はご存知だと思います。
もし分からなければ、ご連絡ください。
データに関してもご質問があれば、聞いてください。

---

## Words and Phrases

| | |
|---|---|
| □求める、願う | request |
| □残念ながら | unfortunately |
| □〜する時間がありません | I don't have enough time to do 〜 |
| □すみませんが、〜 | I'm sorry to say that 〜 |
| □〜できません | It is impossible to 〜 |

## Useful Expressions
## 応用表現

### 依頼を受ける

□喜んでお手伝いします。
  I'm glad to help.

□いいですよ！
  Sure!

□まったく問題ないですよ！
  No problem at all!

□すぐに処理します。
  I'll take care of this right away.

□ご依頼のデータを送ります。
  Here is the data you requested.

### 条件つきで依頼を受ける

□喜んでお手伝いしますが、来週の火曜までは始められません。それでもよろしいですか。
  I'm happy to help you, but I can't get started until next Tuesday. Is that okay?

□今日はその仕事をするのは不可能です。

It's impossible to do that job today.

## 依頼を断る

□ご依頼の資料を持っていません。

I don't have the information you requested.

□ABCプロジェクトに追われていますので、ご依頼のデータを送ることができません。

I won't be able to send the data you requested because I'm tied up with the ABC project.

□今年の売上データは、あと1週間しないと用意できません。

The sales data of this year won't be ready for another week.

□今その仕事をする時間がありません。誰か他の人に頼んでいただけませんか。

I don't have enough time to do that job now. Could you ask someone else?

## 依頼の内容を確認する

□あなたが言われる「情報」の意味がよく分かりません。

I'm not sure what you meant by "information."

□依頼内容を詳しく説明していただけますか。

Can you explain your request in detail?

□必要な売上データについて、もう少し具体的に教えていただけますか。

Can you be more specific about the sales data you need?

□どのデータのことですか。

Which data are you talking about?

□いつまでにそのデータが必要なのですか。

How soon do you need the data?

**その他**

□これが役に立てばいいのですが。

I hope this helps.

□他に提供できる資料があれば、喜んでお送りします。

If there's any other information I can provide, I'll be happy to send it to you.

---

**【英語表現のていねい度】**

英語表現にもていねいのレベルがあります。

相手や状況によって使い分けましょう。

● 一方的な依頼表現で、立場が上の人から下の人への表現

Please reply by tomorrow.

I'd like you to reply by tomorrow.

● 一般的なていねい表現で、相手を問わず使える表現

Would you mind replying by tomorrow?

Could I ask you to reply by tomorrow?

Could you reply by tomorrow?

Would you reply by tomorrow?

　＊Would (Could) you please 〜?のように "please" をつけるとさら
　　にていねい度が増します。

I would appreciate it if you could reply by tomorrow.

● 非常にていねいな表現

Would it be possible for you to reply by tomorrow?

I was wondering if you could reply by tomorrow.

## ③依頼に対するお礼

一言でもよいので、依頼に対応してくれたお礼を伝えておきましょう。

Subject: Thank you for your help

Dear Tracy:

Thank you very much for the data.
Actually, I didn't know how to expand the file, but my assistant helped me.
The data was just what I wanted to know.
It was very helpful.
Thank you!

件名：助けてくれてありがとう

トレイシー様

データの件、本当にありがとう。
実は、解凍の仕方を知らなかったのですが、アシスタントが手伝ってくれました。
まさに私が欲しかったデータでした。
とても役立ちました。
どうもありがとう！

## Words and Phrases

□感謝する                        appreciate

□〜をありがとうございます          Thank you for 〜

## Useful Expressions
### 応用表現

□ご協力いただき、ありがとうございます。
Thank you for your cooperation.

□助けていただき、ありがとうございます。
Thank you for your assistance.

□手配していただき、ありがとうございます。
Thank you for your arrangement.

□お時間をいただき、どうもありがとうございます。
Thank you very much for your time.

□貴重な情報をありがとうございます。
Thank you for the valuable information.

□ご助力に感謝します。
I appreciate your help.

□あなたからの情報はとても助かりました。
Your information was very helpful.

□あなたが昨日送信してくださったデータは、まさに私が知りたかったものです。
The data you sent me yesterday was just what I wanted to know.

# 2. 通　　知

最近では、会議開催の通知など、通知がメールで行われるようになりました。
通知内容は、なるべく簡潔にまとめましょう。

Subject: The monthly meeting

To whom it may concern:

The next monthly meeting is scheduled for :
Monday, July 1st, 9:00 a.m. in the meeting room.

Agenda: Sales strategy of our new product

Please make arrangements so that all those concerned will be
present.
Please let me know by June 25th if you cannot attend.

件名：月例会議

関係者各位

次回月例会議は次のように予定されています。
7月1日　月曜日　午前9時　会議室にて

議題：新商品の販売戦略

関係者全員が出席できるよう調整してください。
出席できない場合は、6月25日までに知らせてください。

## Words and Phrases

| | |
|---|---|
| □議題 | agenda |
| □会議の目的 | the purpose of the meeting |
| □〜について話し合う | discuss 〜 |
| □詳細 | details |

## Useful Expressions
### 応用表現

**会議開催の通知**

□会議の目的は、新製品の価格設定です。

The purpose of the meeting is the pricing of our new products.

□会議は午後4時スタートです。

The meeting starts at 4:00 p.m.

□会議の前に、添付したデータに目を通しておいてください。

Please look over the attached data before the meeting.

□広告戦略について議論します。

We will discuss the advertising strategy.

□会議では、田中さんが幕張でのEXPO2003の報告をします。

At the meeting, Mr.Tanaka will report on the EXPO2003 in Makuhari.

□詳細は、後ほどEメールにてお知らせいたします。

For the details, I'll let you know by e-mail later.

□会議の詳細は、掲示板に掲載します。

I'll put the details of the meeting on the bulletin board.

□会議についての質問があれば、お問い合わせください。

Please contact me if you have any questions regarding the meeting.

□健康診断が5月中旬にあります。

We will have a medical examination in the middle of May.

□明日は棚卸のため閉店します。

We will be closed for inventory tomorrow.

□メンテナンスのため工場は閉鎖されます。

Our factory will be closed for maintenance.

□7月1日から8月31日の間で1週間の休暇を取れます。

You can take a week's vacation from July 1st through August 31st.

□レポートの提出期限は7月5日です。

The deadline of this paper is July 5th.

□明日の朝、社長が当社の品質マネジメントシステムをチェックしに来ます。

The president will come here to check our quality management system tomorrow morning.

**その他の通知**

□3月10日の土曜日に、ポットラックパーティを開催します。

We'll be having a potluck party on Saturday, March 10th.

□3月5日までに、出席するかどうか知らせてください。

Please let me know by March 5th whether you are attending or not.

□12月20日にパーティを企画しています。そのパーティに、とても有名なマジシャンであるMr.モリーをスペシャルゲストとして招く予定です。

We're planning to have a party on December 20th. Mr. Morry, a very famous magician, will be a special guest at the party.

□来たる土曜日に相模川の川原でバーベキューパーティを開こうと思います。

We'd like to have a BBQ party at the riverside of the Sagami River this coming Saturday.

# 3．出張手配

## ①出張手配の依頼

出張の手配を依頼するときには、出張期間や人数、また希望のホテルなどがある場合はその旨を伝えておきましょう。

---

Subject: Request to reserve a room

Dear Jocelyn:

As you know, I will be traveling to Paris during the exposition next month. Could you please reserve a single room at a hotel near the Charles-de-Gaulle International Airport?

Check in : July 12th
Check out : July 16th
I prefer a non-smoking room.

Please let me know the confirmation number when you reserve a room.
Thank you.

---

件名：部屋の予約依頼

ジャスリン様

ご存知の通り、来月開催の博覧会の間、パリに出張します。
シャルルドゴール国際空港の近くのホテルにシングルを一部屋予約し
ていただけませんか。

チェックイン：7月12日
チェックアウト：7月16日
禁煙の部屋を希望します。

予約時の予約番号を教えてください。
よろしくお願いいたします。

## Words and Phrases

| | |
|---|---|
| □予約する | reserve／book |
| □〜を好む | prefer |
| □宿泊設備 | accommodation |
| □喫煙の | smoking |
| □禁煙の | non-smoking |
| □手配する | make an arrangement |
| □（宿泊）設備 | accommodation |
| □交通機関 | transportation |
| □出張 | business trip |
| □現地調査 | field trip |
| □出張する | go on a business trip／go out of town on business／go away on business |
| □海外出張に行く | travel abroad on business |

# Useful Expressions

## 応用表現

□佐々木氏と私は、来月そちらに出張いたします。

Mr. Sasaki and I will visit you next month.

□9月5日から18日までボストンに出張します。

I will be in Boston from September 5th through 18th.

□8月10日にそちらに伺います。

I'll be visiting you on August 10th.

□8月10日からニューヨークに行きます。

I'll be in New York from August 10th.

□佐々木潤と私は、8月10日（月）から8月15日（土）までパリに行きます。

Jun Sasaki and I will be in Paris from Monday, August 10th through Saturday, August 15th.

□飛行機のスケジュールは次の通りです。

My flight schedule is as follows:

8月10日午後4時　成田発（AA001便）

August 10th 4:00 p.m. Lv. Narita (AA001)

8月10日午前9時　サンフランシスコ着

August 10th 9:00 a.m. Ar. San Francisco

### 宿泊・交通手段の手配を頼む

□宿泊の手配をしていただけないでしょうか。

Could you please make arrangements for hotel accommodations?

□ご手配いただければ幸いです。

I'd appreciate it if you could make the arrangements.

□ABCホテルに、シングルの予約をしていただければ幸いです。
  I'd appreciate it if you could reserve a single room at the ABC Hotel.

□シングルの部屋を4泊予約していただけるととても助かります。
  It would be very helpful if you could reserve a single room for four nights.

□11月13日〜20日までの宿泊の予約をお願いしたいのですが。
  I'd like you to reserve a hotel from November 13th to 20th.

□本社の近くのホテルに宿泊したいのです。
  I'd like to stay at the hotel near the head office.

□ABCホテルかXYZホテルがいいのですが。
  I'd prefer either ABC Hotel or XYZ Hotel.

□コンベンションセンターの近くのホテルに宿泊したいのです。
  I'd like to stay at the hotel near the Convention Center.

□東京発ロンドン行きの片道航空券を1枚予約してください。
  Please reserve a one-way ticket from Tokyo to London.

□シカゴ滞在中、車を借りたいのです。
  I'd like to rent a car during my stay in Chicago.

□そこでレンタカーも借りてもらいたいのですが。
  I'd also like you to rent a car there.

□小型車がよいのですが。
  I'd prefer a compact car.

### 感謝の意を述べる

□お手伝いいただき感謝いたします。
  I'd appreciate your help.

□お手伝いいただきありがとうございます。
  Thank you for your help.

□よろしくお願いいたします。

Thank you in advance.

□ご助力ありがとうございます。

Thank you for your help.

## その他

□予約番号を控えておいてください。

Please note the reservation number.

□他のホテルを紹介していただけませんか。

Could you recommend any other hotels?

□料金が分かれば教えてください。

Please tell me the rate if you know.

□成田からホテルまでの行き方を教えてください。

Please tell me how to get to the hotel from Narita.

# ②出張手配の依頼に対する返事

出張の手配ができたら、その情報を間違いがないように伝えます。希望どおりに手配できなかった場合は、代案を用意しておきましょう。

## 依頼への返事

Subject: Re: Request to reserve a room

Dear Philip:

I reserved two single rooms for four nights at the Brilliant Hotel.
Please check in on October 17th starting at 3:00 p.m. and check
out on October 21st by 10:00 p.m.
I'll fax you a map of the city in a few days.
If you have any questions, please e-mail me at
watanabe@abc.com

件名：Re: 部屋の予約依頼

フィリップ様

ブリリアントホテルにシングル2部屋を4泊分予約しました。
10月17日午後3時以降にチェックインし、10月21日午前10時までにチェックアウトしてください。
近日中に市内の地図をファックスします。
ご質問がございましたら、watanabe@abc.comまでEメールでご連絡ください。

## 依頼に添えなかった場合の返事

Subject: URGENT: Please let me know ASAP

Dear Philip:

I tried to reserve a single room for one night on June 20th at the ABC Hotel.
Unfortunately, all the single rooms are full for that day.
A twin room is available, though.
It's ¥10,000 plus a 10% service charge for a night.
Would you like me to reserve a twin room at the ABC Hotel or to try any other hotels?

Please let me know as soon as possible.

---

件名：緊急：至急ご連絡ください

フィリップ様

ABCホテルに6月20日から1泊でシングルの部屋を予約してみました。
残念ながら、シングルの部屋は満室でした。
ツインの部屋であれば空いているのですが。
1泊1万円と10%のサービス料がかかります。
ABCホテルにツインの部屋を予約しますか？それとも他のホテルをあたってみましょうか？

できるだけ早くご連絡ください。

## Useful Expressions
## 応用表現

**予約したことを伝える**

□ABCホテルに2泊シングルの部屋を予約いたしました。

We've reserved a single room at the ABC Hotel for two nights.

□佐々木潤の名前でホテルを予約いたしました。

A hotel reservation has been made under the name of Jun Sasaki.

□10月14日の予約は完了いたしました。

Your reservation of October 14th has been completed.

□シングルを5泊分予約しました。

We have reserved a single room for five nights.

□喫煙の部屋を予約しました。

We have reserved a smoking room.

□交通機関を手配しました。

I made arrangements for transportation.

## 予約できなかったことを伝える

☐あなたがご希望だったホテルは、7月14日は全室満室です。

All rooms of the hotel you requested are booked up on July 14th.

☐プリンセスホテルでは今のところ空き部屋はありません。

The Princess Hotel has no vacancies at present.

☐12月24日はクリスマスイヴのため、予約できませんでした。

I couldn't make a reservation on December 24th because of Christmas Eve.

## 情報を伝える

☐宿泊料金は、1泊7,500円で、税別です。

The room rate is ¥7,500 plus tax per night.

☐宿泊料金は、税込みで1万円です。

The room rate is ¥10,000 including tax.

☐宿泊料金は、朝食込みで1万円です。

The room rate is ¥10,000 including breakfast.

☐ドゴールホテルの情報は次の通りです。

The information for De Gaulle Hotel is as follows:

☐ホテルは、新宿駅より徒歩3分です。

The hotel is a three-minute walk from Shinjuku Station.

☐ドゴールホテルのURLです。

Here is the URL of the De Gaulle Hotel.

☐ホテルは本社の近くにあります。

The hotel is located near the head office.

☐チェックインは午後3時からで、チェックアウトは午前10時となっています。

Check-in time is 3:00 p.m., and check-out time is 10:00 a.m.

□ホテルは、成田国際空港の近くにあります。
The hotel is located near Narita International Airport.

□空港から東京ホテルまでの一番便利な行き方は、シャトルバスです。
The most convenient way to get to the hotel from the airport is by shuttle bus.

## その他

□ご質問がありましたら、お気軽にお問い合わせください。
Please feel free to ask me any questions.

□お手伝いできることがあれば、お知らせください。
Please let me know if I can help you.

□ご到着をお待ちしております。
We look forward to your arrival.

□来週お目にかかるのを楽しみにしています。
We're looking forward to seeing you next week.

□成田空港へお迎えに参ります。
I will pick you up at the airport.

□スケジュールの変更がございましたら、お知らせください。
If there are any changes in your schedule, please let me know.

# ③出張の変更の知らせと再手配の依頼

出張日程が変更になってしまった場合は、相手に手間をかけることを詫び、再度手配してもらいましょう。

---

Subject: Change of my schedule

Dear Jocelyn:

My schedule has been changed after the meeting with Mr. Nakamura, our Sales Manager.

My departure date has changed from November 30th to December 1st because I have to attend the monthly sales meeting instead of him.
I'll return on December 5th as I told you.
So, I'd like you to cancel the hotel reservation for November 30th.

I'm very sorry to trouble you.

---

件名：スケジュールの変更

ジャスリン様

私のスケジュールが営業部長である中村氏とのミーティングの後、変更になりました。

中村氏の代わりに月例営業会議に出席しなければならないため、出発日が11月30日から12月1日に変更になりました。
帰りは申し上げたとおり12月5日です。
というわけで、11月30日のホテルをキャンセルしていただきたいのです。

お手数をおかけして本当にすみません。

---

## Words and Phrases

| | |
|---|---|
| □変更する | change |
| □キャンセルする | cancel |
| □延期になる | postpone |

## Useful Expressions
### 応用表現

**予定の変更を伝える**

□私の出張はキャンセルになりました。
My trip has been canceled.

□アメリカへの出張を1週間延期しなければならなくなりそうです。
I'll have to postpone my trip to the U.S. for a week.

□出張計画を計画し直さなければならなくなりました。
I have to reschedule my travel plans.

□スケジュールが変更になりました。
My schedule has been changed.

**予約の変更を依頼する**

□予約を3月1日から3月3日に変更していただけますか。
Could you change my reservation from March 1st to March 3rd?

□ホテルをグランドホテルに変更していただきたいのです。
I'd like you to change the hotel to the Grand Hotel.

□後ほど、ホテルの予約をお願いします。
I'll ask you to reserve a hotel room later.

## 迷惑をかけたことを詫びる

□お手数をおかけしてすみません。
I'm sorry to trouble you.

□ごめんなさい。
Sorry about that.

【つなぎの英語表現】

| | |
|---|---|
| さて | Well |
| ご存知のとおり | As you know |
| とにかく | Anyway |
| ところで | By the way |
| 言い換えれば | In other words |
| まず | First of all |
| 最後に | Finally |
| 私の知る限りでは | As far as I know |
| 私の意見では | In my opinion |

# ④出張前の確認

出張前に、手配内容を確認しておくことも大切です。

Subject: Confirmation of my flight schedule

Dear George:

I'd like to confirm your flight schedule regarding your visit in June.
－June 10th 11:30 a.m. Ar. LAX ABC080
－June 28th 2:00 p.m. Lv. LAX ABC197

If there are any changes in your flight schedule, please let me know.
We look forward to seeing you.

件名：飛行機のスケジュールの確認

ジョージ様

6月の来社に関して、飛行機のスケジュールを確認したいのです。
・6月10日午前11時30分LAX着、ABC080便
・6月28日午後2時LAX発、ABC197便

スケジュールの変更がございましたら、ご連絡ください。
お目にかかれることを楽しみにしています。

## Words and Phrases

□確認する　　　　　　make sure／confirm

# Useful Expressions
## 応用表現

**確　認**

□ホテルの予約の確認をしていただけませんか。

Could you confirm my hotel reservation?

□飛行機のスケジュールは次の通りです。

My flight schedule is as follows:

**その他**

□5月25日にお目にかかるのを楽しみにしております。

I am looking forward to seeing you on May 25th.

□新宿駅に着きましたらお電話ください。

Please call me when you arrive at Shinjuku Station.

□銀座駅のA3出口で、黒いスーツを着てシルバーの眼鏡をかけてお待ちしております。

I'll be waiting for you at exit A3 in Ginza Station, and I'll be wearing a black suit and silver glasses.

□私の携帯番号をお教えしておきます：090－1234－5678

I give you my cellular phone number: 090-1234-5678

□もし差し支えなければ、携帯番号と携帯電話のEメールアドレスを教えてください。

Please let me know the number and e-mail address of your cellular phone, if you don't mind.

□お気をつけてお越しください。

Have a safe trip.

# 4. コミュニケーション

社内の人に対しても、一緒に仕事をしていく上で、コミュニケーションをとることが大切です。

---

Subject: Request for reserving a meeting room

Dear James:

How's your new project going?
I hope you're doing well.

I'd like to reserve a meeting room at 9:00 a.m. on May 5th.
Please let me know if it's available.

Have a nice weekend!

---

件名：会議室の予約依頼

ジェームス様

新プロジェクトの進み具合はどうですか？
順調だと良いのですが。

5月5日の午前9時に会議室を予約したいのですが。
利用可能かどうか、お知らせください。

良い週末を！

# Useful Expressions
## 応用表現

**近況を尋ねる**

□元気ですか？
　How're you doing?

□相変わらず忙しいですか？
　Are you busy as usual?

□良い週末でしたか？
　Did you have a nice weekend?

□しばらく会っていませんね。
　I haven't seen you for a while.

**【仕事の進捗】**
□仕事の具合はいかがですか？
　How's your job going?

□プレゼンテーションは終わりましたか？
　Have you finished your presentation yet?

□9月の売上げはどうでしたか。
　How were sales for September?

□企画書を拝見したいのですが。
　I'd like to take a look at your proposal.

**近況を伝える**

□こちらは順調です。
　I'm doing well.

□こちらは相変わらずです。
　Things have been the same here.

207

□最近とても忙しいです。
　I've been very busy recently.

□最近、出張続きです。
　I've been traveling a lot.

□休みを取りたいです。
　I want to have a holiday.

□ストレスがたまっています。
　I'm stressed out.

□イタリア旅行のことでわくわくしています。
　I'm so excited about my trip to Italy.

□夏休みにヨーロッパに旅行に行ってきました。
　I took a trip to Europe for summer vacation.

**【仕事の進捗】**
□現在、大きなプロジェクトに取り組んでいます。
　I'm currently working on a big project.

□来週には新しい仕事に取り掛かることができるといいのですが。
　I hope we can start new work next week.

□ひとつ問題がありまして、解決するのに2〜3日かかりそうです。
　There's a problem, and it may take a few days to solve.

## 最後にひとこと

□無理しないでね。
　Don't work too much.

□お大事に！
　Take care!

□また後ほど！
　Talk to you later!

□明日会いましょう！
See you tomorrow!

その他

□明日お休みします。
I'll be off tomorrow.

□ 明日は午後から出社します。
I'll be in the office tomorrow afternoon.

□成瀬さんが、折り返し電話をいただきたいとのことでした。
Ms. Naruse left you a message that she'd like you to call her back.

□明日正午までに、この問題を解決できますか？
Will it be possible to solve this problem by tomorrow noon?

□来週までにABCソフトの開発が終わるかどうか教えてください。
Please tell me if you can finish developing the ABC software by next week.

□来週の金曜日の会議で、新ソフトについてプレゼンテーションをしていただきたいのですが。
I would like you to make a presentation about our new software in the meeting next Friday.

□ご協力いただきましてありがとうございます。
Thank you for your cooperation.

□会議の日程を変更してもらえませんか。明日は外出する予定です。
Is it possible to change the date of the meeting?  I'll be out tomorrow.

□午後3時からプロジェクタをお借りできますか。
Is it possible to use the projector from 3:00 p.m.?

□昨日いただいた質問には、後程回答いたします。
I'll get back to you later about the question you asked me yesterday.

□今週末、村井さんのお宅でのランチパーティーに参加しますか。

Are you coming to the lunch party at Mr. Murai's house this weekend?

□できるだけ早く、パソコンのチェックをしてください。昨日、あなたからウィルスに感染したメールが届きましたよ。

Please check your computer as soon as possible. Yesterday, I received an e-mail from you infected by a virus.

□MM社へ行くときには、この請求書を持っていってください。

When you go to MM Company, please take this invoice with you.

**3** | **Eメールでよく使われる表現**

# 1. 添付ファイル

## 添付ファイルを送る

□このメッセージにテキストファイルを添付します。
  I am attaching a text file to this message.

□添付いたしましたのは、ご依頼がございました弊社の最新版のカタログです。
  Attached is our latest catalog that you requested.

□2種類の形式でファイルを添付します。
  I am attaching files in two kinds of format.

□これはマイクロソフトワードのファイルです。
  This is a Microsoft Word file.

## 添付ファイルに関するトラブル

□添付ファイルを開くことができません。
  I cannot open the attached file.

□添付画像ファイルを開くことができません。
  I cannot open the attached photo file.

□添付ファイルの開き方を教えてください。
  Please tell me how to open the attachment.

□添付ファイルを開くのに、特別なソフトウェアが必要ですか。
  Do I need particular software to open the attachment?

□マイクロソフトワードを持っていません。
  I don't have Microsoft Word.

II

機能別Eメールサンプル・表現集

□テキスト形式のファイルを送っていただけますか。
  Could you send a file in text format?

□テキストファイルを送ってください。
  Please send a text file.

□ファイルが読めませんでした。
  The file was unreadable.

□私のコンピュータでは添付ファイルが読めません。
  I cannot read the attachment on my computer.

□私のコンピュータで韓国語は読めません。
  I can't read Korean characters on my computer.

□私はウィンドウズを使っています。
  I use Windows.

□このファイルが作られたソフトウェアが、私のコンピュータにインストールされていません。
  The software this file was made with is not installed in my computer.

# 2．メールの転送

□顧客からのメールを転送します。
  I am forwarding the e-mail from our client.

□このメールを営業担当者に転送していただけますか。
  Could you forward this e-mail to the proper person in charge of sales?

□あなたのメールを弊社カスタマーサービス部門へ転送いたしました。
  Your e-mail has been forwarded to our customer service department.

# 3. 圧縮・解凍

□添付ファイルは圧縮されています。
The attached file is compressed.

□ファイルを解凍してください。
Please expand the file.

□添付ファイルは解凍してください。
Please expand the attachment.

# 4. メール送受信時のトラブル

□あなたに送ったEメールが戻ってきました。
The e-mail I sent you came back.

□メッセージを送ることができませんでした。
I couldn't send any messages.

□受信中に何らかのトラブルがあったようです。
There might have been an error during transmission.

□間違ったアドレスにEメールを送信されています。
You sent the e-mail to the wrong address.

□私のコンピュータが壊れました。
My computer was broken down.

□私のコンピュータがフリーズしていました。
My computer froze.

□弊社のサーバーがダウンしていました。
Our server was down.

# 5．その他

□マイクロソフトエクセルをお持ちですか。

Do you have Microsoft Excel?

□どのブラウザソフトをお使いですか。

What browser software do you use?

□ボックスメニューの「アプリケーションから開く」をクリックしてください。

Please click on the "Open from Application" in the box menu.

□インターネットからそのソフトをダウンロードできます。

You can download the software from the Internet.

□昨日お送りしたファイルを削除してください。

Please delete the file that I sent you yesterday.

□添付したデータがお役に立てば幸いです。

I hope the attached data is helpful.

# Ⅲ

## ホームページで
## よく使う表現

# 1. トップページ

■Home
■What's new!
■Products
■Info Request
■About ABC
■Career
■Contact Us

**Your Business Partner Since 2001**

**ABC Corporation**

Copyright© 2001 ABC Corporation. All rights reserved.

■ホームページ
■新着情報！
■製品案内
■資料請求
■ABC社について
■採用情報
■お問い合わせ

**２００１年以来、貴社のビジネスパートナー**

**ＡＢＣ社**

著作権　２００１年ABC社

## Words and Phrases

| | |
|---|---|
| □新着情報 | what's new |
| □最新情報 | the latest information |
| □会社概要 | about 会社名／about us |
| □会社案内 | company profile／corporate profile／company overview |
| □主要業務 | major products and services |
| □事業内容 | about our products and services／business |
| □商品〔サービス〕案内 | products (services) ／our products (services) |
| □情報 | information |
| □技術情報 | technology information |
| □財務状況 | financial status |
| □投資家関連情報 | investor relations／investor information |
| □投資家の皆様へ、投資家情報 | for investors |
| □ABCの株主様への情報 | information for ABC's shareholders |
| □株式情報 | stock information |
| □年次報告書 | annual report |
| □購入 | purchase |
| □注文 | order |
| □採用 | career／job |
| □資料請求 | information request |
| □よくある質問 | FAQs. (=Frequently Asked Questions) |
| □無料資料 | free materials |
| □国内拠点 | domestic offices |
| □海外拠点 | overseas offices |
| □サイトマップ | site map |

| | |
|---|---|
| □トップページ | top page |
| □リンク | link |
| □問い合わせ先 | contact us |
| □プライバシーに関して | privacy statement |
| □最終更新日 | last updated |
| □最終更新日：2003年9月20日 | last modified: September 20th, 2003 |
| □2003年9月20日現在 | as of September 20th, 2003 |

## Useful Expressions
### 応用表現

□当社のウェブサイトへようこそ！

Welcome to our web site!

□世界中のお客様を歓迎します。

We are pleased to welcome all international customers.

□弊社の新製品をご覧になりたい方は、ここをクリック！

Click here to see our new product!

□特別キャンペーン情報、新サービス情報などなど···。

Information on special campaigns, new services, and more...

□下のリンクにより、複数の言語で情報が閲覧できます。

Information is available in multiple languages, via the links below:

□このサイトは http://www.aaa.com に移動しました。

This site was moved to http://www.aaa.com

□ブックマークを更新してください。

Please update your bookmarks.

□このページは現在制作中です。前ページに戻るには、戻るボタンを使用してください。

This page is currently under construction.  Please use your back button to return to the previous page.

## 会員ページへのログイン

□このページにアクセスする前にサインインしてください。

You must sign in before you access this page.

□IDとパスワードを入力してください。

Please enter your ID and password.

□ユーザーIDとパスワードを入力し、「SIGN IN」ボタンをクリックしてください。

Please enter your user ID and password, then click on the "SIGN IN" button.

□3回ログインに失敗すると、約30分間ログインできなくなります。

You cannot log in for almost half an hour if you fail to log in three times.

□3回ログインに失敗すると、IDを失うことになります。

If you fail to log in three times, you lose your ID.

□下の「BACK」ボタンで戻り、問題を修正してください。

Please use the "BACK" button below to go back and correct the problem.

□このページを見るには、会員である必要があります。

You have to be a member to view this page.

□今入力されたEメールアドレスは、すでに使われています。

The e-mail address you just entered has already been used for another account.

□確認のためにパスワードを再入力してください。

Please reenter your password to confirm.

□エラー！パスワードが間違っています。

Error! Your password is not correct.

# ２．会社案内

## ①会社概要

ABC Co., Ltd. was established in 1980 in Tokyo, Japan.
We specialize in auto parts and related accessories including headlights, taillights, mirrors, bumpers, doors and more.
We now export our products to over 30 countries worldwide.
Our mission is to provide our customers with the highest quality products.
We emphasize the improvement of our products, as well as new developments of innovative products for the future.

ABC社は1980年に東京に設立されました。
当社は、ヘッドライト、テイルライト、ミラー、バンパー、ドアなどの自動車部品や関連付属品を専門にしております。
当社は現在、製品を世界30ヶ国超に輸出しております。
当社の使命は、顧客に最高品質の製品を提供することです。
当社では、将来に向けた革新的な製品の開発と同時に、製品の改良を重視しています。

# ②沿　革

## History

1995 - Katsumi Yamamoto founds ABC Inc. in Yokohama with the aim of providing Internet service.

1996 - ABC starts total Internet services only for corporate members in collaboration with ABC telecommunication.

1998 - ABC changes its name to ABC Online Inc., and relocates its head office to 1-1-1, Nishi-Shinjuku, Shinjuku-ku.

1999 - ABC starts a consulting service.

2001 - ABC starts an e-Learning service with the aim of further strengthening our consulting business.

2002 - ABC opens the Shibuya Sales Branch.

## 沿　革

1995年 - 山本克美が、インターネットサービスの提供を目的として、ABC社を横浜に設立する。

1996年 - ABCテレコミュニケーションと提携し、法人会員向けの総合インターネットサービスを開始する。

1998年 - 社名をＡＢＣオンライン社に変更し、新宿区西新宿1-1-1に本社を移す。

1999年 - コンサルティングサービスを開始する。

2001年 - コンサルティングビジネスをさらに強化するために、イーラーニングサービスを開始する。

2002年 - 渋谷営業所を開設する。

※沿革を記述する際には、現在形、過去形のどちらも用いられています。
また、例のように箇条書きにまとめている会社もありますが、①会社概要の例のように、文章でまとめている会社も多くみられます。

## Words and Phrases

| | |
|---|---|
| □弊社について | about us／about 会社名／who we are |
| □会社概要 | company profile／corporate profile／company overview |
| □会社名 | company name |
| □本社 | head office |
| □設立 | founded |
| □資本金 | paid-in capital／capital |
| □売上高 | sales |
| □年間売上高 | annual turnover |
| □社長 | president |
| □代表者 | company representative |
| □従業員数 | number of employees |
| □取締役会 | Board of Directors |
| □主要営業品目 | major business lines |
| □主要取引先 | major clients |
| □子会社 | subsidiary（company） |
| □系列会社 | affiliated company |
| □使命、企業目標 | mission statement／our mission |
| □企業理念 | our philosophy |
| □株主 | shareholder |
| □株式情報 | stock information |
| □株式上場 | stock exchange listing |
| □沿革 | （corporate）history |
| □提供する | provide |
| □設立する | establish／found |
| □拡大する | expand |
| □事業 | business |
| □創設者 | founder |
| □顧客リストを閲覧する | view our client list |

| □創立年月日 | date of foundation／date established |
|---|---|
| □基本方針 | our policy |
| □〔新商品を〕売り出す、始める | launch |
| □世界中に | worldwide |
| □特許 | patent |
| □～を目的として設立する | found with the aim of ～ |
| □～に進出する | step into ～ |
| □社名を～と変更する | change the company name to ～ |
| □吸収合併 | merger |

## Useful Expressions
### 応用表現

**会社概要**

□ABC社は、30年間、高品質の不動産サービスをご提供してまいりました。

ABC Corporation has provided real estate services of the highest quality for three decades.

□ABCは、世界的な情報技術サービス会社です。

ABC is a worldwide information technology services company.

□XXXとYYYの合併によってつくられたABCは、世界大手の航空会社です。

ABC, formed by the merger of XXX and YYY, is one of the world's leading airlines.

□ABCは、最大の品揃えの自転車をご提供いたします。

ABC offers the largest selection of bicycles.

□ABC社は、資本金5,000万円で設立された会社です。

ABC Co., Ltd. is a company established with a capital of 50 million yen.

□ABC.comには、20ヶ国に約1,000人の従業員がいます。

ABC.com employs approximately 1,000 people in 20 countries.

□我々の使命は、真のビジネスの問題を解決するような製品を発明することです。

Our mission is to invent products that solve real business problems.

□「品質」は、我々のモットーです。

"Quality First" is our motto.

## 沿 革

□ABCペーパーカンパニーは、間中次郎によって2001年に設立されました。

ABC Paper Company was founded in 2001 by Jiro Manaka.

□ABCは、1800年に数名の社員で創設されました。

ABC was founded in 1800 with a handful of employees.

□ABC社は、1900年に小さな家電会社としてスタートしました。

ABC started in 1900 as a small electric household appliances company.

□1900年にABCが設立されて以来、ウイルス対策ソフトウェアを開発してまいりました。

Since ABC's establishment in 1900, we have developed anti-virus software.

□1990年の創業以来、ABCは最大の衣料品小売業者のひとつに成長してまいりました。

Since its beginning in 1990, ABC has grown into one of the largest apparel retailers.

□銀座にある初店舗をはじめ、ABCは、全国約200店舗にまで拡大しました。

From that first store in Ginza, ABC has expanded to approximately 200 stores nationwide.

□ABCは、日本、フランス、イタリアに500支店以上に拡張してきました。

ABC has expanded to over 500 branches in Japan, France, and Italy.

□ABCは、1992年にフランチャイズ展開を開始しました。

ABC began to franchise its stores in 1992.

□当社は、新サービスである「ドキュメントトランク」を2002年に開始いたしました。

We started our new service "Document Trunk" in 2002.

□ABCは、インターネットを通じてドキュメント管理する「IDS」を発売いたしました。

ABC launched "IDS" to provide document management through the Internet.

□ABCは、東京証券取引所に上場しています。

ABC is listed on the Tokyo Stock Exchange.

**その他**

□さらに情報をお求めの方はご連絡ください。

Please contact us for additional information.

【ホームページについて】
一般に私達が日本語で「ホームページ」と呼んでいるものは、英語では"web site" や "web page" といいます。英語の"home page"はトップページをさします。また、ホームページアドレスのことは"URL"といいます。

## ABC Investor Relations

**□Announcements**
**Financial Results for FY2002 have been released.**

□Financial Information
View the 2002 Annual Report

□Press Releases
□IR Events
□Stock Quotes
□FAQs

## ABCの投資家の皆様へ

**□お知らせ**
**2002年度決算を発表いたしました。**

□財務情報
2002年の年次報告書を見る

□プレスリリース
□IRイベント
□株価動向
□よくある質問

| | |
|---|---|
| □投資家関連情報 | investor relations |
| □株主 | shareholder／stockholder（主に米で使われている） |
| □主な株主 | major shareholders（stockholders） |
| □財務諸表 | financial statement |
| □財務状況 | financial status |
| □年次報告書 | annual report |
| □株 | stock |
| □株価 | stock price |
| □株価情報 | stock quote |
| □普通株 | common stock |
| □年間売上高 | annual turnover |
| □貸借対照表 | balance sheet |
| □損益計算書 | profit and loss statement |
| □報道機関向けの発表 | press release |
| □行事予定一覧 | calendar of events |
| □会計年度 | fiscal year（FYと略記されることが多い） |
| □株主総会 | shareholders' meeting |
| □お知らせ | announcement |
| □前年度 | previous year |
| □連結された | consolidated |
| □四半期 | quarter |
| □通常の | ordinary |
| □臨時の | extraordinary |
| □業績 | business results |
| □社債 | bond |
| □発行する | issue |
| □中期経営計画 | medium-term management plan |

## Useful Expressions

### 応用表現

□2003年度決算発表

Announcement of Financial Results for FY 2003

□第50回定時株主総会

The 50th Ordinary General Meeting of Shareholders

□第50回定時株主総会召集通知を掲載しました（2003年6月10日）。

Notice of convocation of the 50th Ordinary General Meeting of Shareholders posted (June 10th, 2003).

□ABCは2001年4月1日に東京証券取引所に上場いたしました。

ABC was listed on April 1st, 2001 at Tokyo Stock Exchange.

□本サイトの株価情報は、ABCによるものです。

The stock information on this site was prepared by ABC.

□すべてのファイルは、フリーソフトウェアであるアドビアクロバットリーダーが必要なPDF形式となっております。このアプリケーションをお持ちでない方は、下のボタンをクリックしてダウンロードしてください。

All files are in PDF format, requiring free software Adobe Acrobat Reader. If you do not have this application, click on the button below to download it.

# 3．製品・サービス案内

## ①製造・販売業

**メーカー**

---

### Fast Print with ABC Printer!

#### Features

Up to $4800 \times 1200$ color dpi with microscopic droplets as much as 2 picoliters.

Edge-to-edge true borderless photos.


#### Main Specifications

\<Print Speed\> Black  18  ppm  (approximately  3.3  seconds  per page)

Color 12 ppm (approximately 5 seconds per page)

\<Ink\> XY-10 Black Ink Tank, XY-10 color Ink Tank

\<Paper Size\> Letter, A4, A5, B4, B5···

\<Usable Paper\>Plain  Paper,  Envelops,  Glossy  Photo  Paper, Matte Photo Paper···

\<Physical Dimensions\>： 16.0"W×10.0"D×9.0'H

\<Weight\>：9.5 lbs.

\<Power Source\> 120V AC , 60Hz


About "OS Compatibility" and "Standard Interfaces", click on the **Next Page⇒**

About the warranty, see http://www.abc.com/support.htm

---

## ABCプリンタだと印刷が早い！

### 特徴

2ピコリッターほどの微細な小滴で4800×1200dpiまでのカラーを出力できます。

端の端まで境界線のない写真を出力できます。

### 主要仕様

<印刷速度> 白黒…18 ppm（1頁 約3.3秒）

カラー…12 ppm（1頁 約5秒）

<対応インク> XY-10黒インク、XY-10カラーインク

<用紙サイズ> レターサイズ、A4、A5、B4、B5…

<対応用紙> 普通用紙、封筒、光沢写真用紙、マット写真用紙…

<寸法>幅16.0インチ、奥行き10.0インチ、高さ9.0インチ

<重量> 9.5ポンド

<電圧>AC電源120ボルト、60ヘルツ

対応OSや標準インターフェースについては、**Next page** ⇒をクリックしてください。

保証に関してはhttp://www.abc.com/support.htmをご覧ください。

## 販　売

Welcome to Beautiful Flower.com!

Fresh flowers starting at only \$25 with a glass vase FREE!

Select from a wide variety of flowers & gifts that are perfect for every occasion!

- Birthday
- Thank you
- Anniversary
- Get Well
- Business

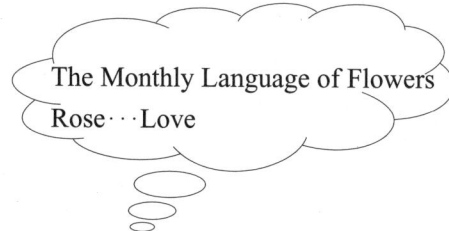

The Monthly Language of Flowers

Rose···Love

Same day delivery available. Order now!

ビューティフル・フラワー・ドットコムにようこそ！

鮮度の高い花が、無料のガラスの花瓶つきで25ドルから！

あらゆる機会に最適な、多種の花とギフトからお選びください！

- 誕生日
- お礼
- 記念日
- お見舞い
- ビジネス

今月の花言葉

バラ…愛

同日配達可能です。今すぐご注文を！

## Words and Phrases

| | |
|---|---|
| □製品 | product |
| □製品情報 | product information |
| □新商品 | new product |
| □最新商品 | the latest product |
| □価格 | price |
| □価格表 | price list |
| □仕様・仕様書 | specifications |
| □値引き | reduction／discount |
| □ダウンロードする | download |
| □お試し商品 | trial ware |
| □検索・検索する | search |
| □詳細検索 | advanced search |
| □検索をしぼりこむ | narrow the search |
| □マニュアル、取扱説明書 | manual |
| □オンラインサービス | online service |
| □カタログ | catalog |
| □標準型 | standard model |
| □保証 | warranty |
| □特徴 | feature |
| □寸法 | dimension／size |
| □重量 | weight |
| □〜からお選びください | select from 〜 |
| □満足を保証します | satisfaction guaranteed |

## Useful Expressions
## 応用表現

**商品情報**

□新製品に関する情報はこちらをクリック。
Click here for information on our new product.

□新サービスの詳細については、次のURLをご参照ください。
Please refer to the following URL for further details of our new services.

□ABCは、月々の契約内で、全ての部品の交換・修理を承っております。
ABC will be responsible for the replacement and repair of all parts under monthly contract.

□弊社のバスルームアクセサリーは、丈夫なプラスチックでできています。
Our bathroom accessories are made of durable plastics.

□これらのサービスが中小企業にも適用されるようになりました。
These services are now available to small and mid-sized companies.

□ABCのウィルス定義の最新版をダウンロードしてください。
Download the latest certified virus definition for ABC.

**商品検索**

□製品名が分からない場合は、左の製品タイプから検索してください。
If you don't know the product name, search by the product type to the left.

□製品名が分かる場合は、下の全製品のリストから選んでください。
If you know the product name, select from the list of all products below.

## 資料請求

□AA型のカタログをご希望の方は、下記アドレスまでご連絡ください。

If you would like to have a catalog of the model AA, please contact us at the following address.

□カタログご請求のお客様には、最新のカタログ、価格表等を送付させていただきます。

If you require a catalog of our products, we will send the latest catalog, price list and so on.

## プロモーション

□オンライン購入の場合は、5%の割引きをいたします。

We will give a reduction of 5% to orders online.

□この期間にお買い上げの場合は、10%の割引きをいたします。

We will give a reduction of 10% to orders during this period.

## 商品サンプル

□「DOWNLOAD」ボタンをクリックすると、無料お試し版をダウンロードできます。

Click on the "DOWNLOAD" button, and you can get a trial version for free.

□ダウンロードしたい場合は、MSワードが必要となります。

If you would like to download, you will need MS-Word.

□サンプルソフトを普通郵便で郵送することもできます。

We can also send the sample software by snail mail.

□次の資料は無料です。

The following materials are free:

□まずはお試しください！

Just try it!

## 注 文

□注文書はここをクリック。

　Click here for an order form.

□弊社の全商品をオンラインストアでご購入いただけます。

　You can buy all of our products from our online store.

## その他

□2つ以上選択する場合は、「ctrl」を押したまま、マウスをクリックしてください。

　To select two or more, hold down "ctrl" key while clicking mouse.

□必ず気に入っていただけるでしょう！

　YOU WILL LIKE IT!

　＊全文を大文字にして強調しています。

# ②サービス業（旅行会社）

## Where would you like to go?
Enter city names. Click "City List" to select from a list.

From : [＿＿＿＿＿＿]        To : [＿＿＿＿＿＿]

⦿ City List                    ⦿ City List

## When would you like to travel?

Depart: [＿＿＿＿＿＿]        Return: [＿＿＿＿＿＿]

## How many passengers are traveling?

Total number of travelers: [＿＿＿＿＿＿]

How many are under 12? [＿＿＿＿＿＿]

## Do you have any preferences?

Airline: [＿＿＿＿＿＿]

Class: ○Economy ○Business ○First class

[ Search now ]        [ Cancel ]

236

どこに行きたいですか？

都市名を入力してください。リストからの選択は "City List" をクリックしてください。

出発地 [　　　　　　]　　　　到着地 [　　　　　　]
　　⦿City List　　　　　　　　⦿City List

旅行予定はいつですか？

出発日 [　　　　　　]　　　　帰国日 [　　　　　　]

旅行人数は何名ですか？

全体人数は？ [　　　　　　]
12歳未満は何名ですか？ [　　　　　　]

ご希望はありますか？

航空会社： [　　　　　　]
クラス：○エコノミー　○ビジネス　○ファーストクラス

[ 検索する ]　　　[ キャンセルする ]

## Words and Phrases

| | |
|---|---|
| □予約 | reservation |
| □予約する | reserve／book |
| □確認する | confirm |
| □レンタカーを借りる | rent a car |
| □荷物 | baggage（主に米）／luggage（主に英） |
| □地図 | map |
| □ガイドブック | guidebook |
| □フライト、飛行機便 | flight |
| □片道 | one way |
| □往復 | round-trip |
| □出発 | departure |
| □到着 | arrival |
| □目的地 | destination |
| □支払方法 | how to pay |

## Useful Expressions
### 応用表現

**予 約**

□席を予約するには赤いボタンをクリックしてください。
　When you reserve a seat, please click on the red button.

□フォームに記入し、下のアイコンをクリックしてください。予約が完了します。
　Please fill out the forms and click on the icon below. Your reservation
　will be completed.

□予約が完了しました！
　Your reservation has been completed!

□予約は完了していません。
　Your reservation has not been completed.

□残念ですが、選択されたホテルは満室です。

Unfortunately, the hotel that you selected is booked up.

□予約の再確認を1週間以内に行ってください。

Please reconfirm the reservation within a week.

## 必要事項

### 【宿泊】

□どこに宿泊したいですか。

Where would you like to stay?

□いつ宿泊しますか。

When will you stay?

□何か特別なアメニティーが必要ですか。

Do you require any special amenities?

□何か特別な設備が必要ですか（3つまで選択できます）。

Do you require any special equipment? (select up to 3 options)

□「Ctrl」キーを押しながらクリックすると、複数のホテルを選択することができます。

By holding down the "Ctrl" key while clicking, you can select multiple hotels.

□下にあるアイテムから選択すると、検索をお好みのホテルに限定します。

Selecting items below will restrict your search to only hotels with the specified preferences.

□タクシーをご用命の場合は、事前にお申し付けください。

Please let us know in advance if you want to use a taxi.

## 【飛行機】

□ 「City List」ボタンをクリックして、空港がある都市リストから選択してください。

Click on the "City List" button to select from a list of cities with airport.

□ どの航空会社を使用しますか。

Which airline do you want to take?

## 【その他】

□ 特別なご希望はありますか。

Do you have any special preferences?

□ どこでレンタカーを借りたいですか。

Where would you like to rent a car?

### 注意事項

□ お部屋代金の10%をサービス料として頂戴しております。

10 % of room charge is included as service.

□ 選択されたオプションに追加料金がかかることもあります。

Additional charges may apply for the options you select.

□ サービス料金は含まれています。

The service price is included.

### 問い合わせ関連

□ パンフレットのご請求は、次のアドレスまでEメールでお問い合わせください。

If you require a brochure, e-mail us at the following address:

□ 期間を延長したい場合は、お近くの店舗までお問い合わせください。

If you want to prolong the period, please contact the nearest shop.

□ 他の部屋の予約を希望される場合は、すぐにお知らせください。

If you would like to reserve an alternative room, please let us know immediately.

□まだご質問がありますか？ FAQのページをご覧ください。

Still have questions? Visit our frequently asked questions page.

## その他

□ガイドブック情報、地図、気象情報、写真等をご覧になって旅行を計画してください。

Plan your trip with guidebook information, maps, weather information, photos, and more.

□ABCホテルグループのホームページから行う予約はすべて、インターネットで有効な最低価格でのご提供となります。

Every hotel reservation booked through an ABC Hotels Group web site is guaranteed to have the lowest rate available on the Internet.

□特別装備は全ての車、全ての場所で利用可能な訳ではありません。

Special equipment may not be available on all cars and all locations.

□直接のご予約に関しては、予約金はいただいておりません。

We do not charge any booking fees for making reservations directly with us.

□お客様よりいただいた全ての個人情報は、安全に保護されています。

All personal information you provide is encrypted and secure.

## 【宿泊関連とレンタカー関連の英語表現】

インターネットで見かける「宿泊関連」と「レンタカー関連」の表現をまとめてみました。

### ＊＊宿泊関連＊＊

| | |
|---|---|
| □レストラン | Restaurant |
| □フィットネスセンター | Fitness Center |
| □ミーティング施設 | Meeting Facilities |
| □子供向けプログラム | Children's Program |
| □ペット可／不可 | Pets Allowed／Not Allowed |
| □ドライクリーニング | Dry Cleaning |
| □車椅子使用可 | Wheelchair Accessible |
| □空室検索と予約 | Room Search and Reservation |
| □料金一覧 | Price List |

### ＊＊レンタカー関連＊＊

| | |
|---|---|
| □チャイルドシート | Child Safety Seat |
| □スキーラック | Ski Rack |
| □チェーン | Snow Chains |
| □自転車ラック | Bicycle Rack |
| □カセット／ＭＤプレーヤー | Cassette／MD Player |
| □右ハンドル | Right hand control |
| □左ハンドル | Left hand control |
| □荷物ラック | Luggage Rack |
| □携帯電話 | Mobile Phone／Cellular Phone |
| □ナビゲーションシステム | Navigational System |
| □乗車場所 | Pick-up City |
| □乗車場所と異なる場合の、乗捨場所 | Drop-off City if different than a pick-up city |

## *Emerald*
### *Bay Tower 42 F*

Emerald presents spectacular views for you to enjoy while relaxing.

There is a special lunchtime menu.
A variety of desserts and beverages are available in the afternoon. And in the evening, you can enjoy wines and cuisine with live music.

At Emerald, you can find a warm and welcoming atmosphere and we believe that you will enjoy our cuisine!

( MENU )   ( Open : 11:00 a.m.~3:00 p.m. Lunch & Afternoon
5:00 p.m.~11:00 p.m. Dinner )

## エメラルド
### Bay Tower 42階

エメラルドでは、リラックスしながら、素晴らしい景色が楽しめます。

特別なランチタイムメニューをご用意しております。
午後は、様々なデザートとお飲み物を、そして夜は、ライブ音楽を聞きながら、ワインや料理をお楽しみいただけます。

エメラルドでは、暖かく歓迎する雰囲気を感じていただけます。私達の料理をお楽しみいただけることを確信しております！

( メニュー )   ( 営業時間：11:00 a.m.~3:00 p.m. ランチ＆アフタヌーン
5:00 p.m.~11:00 p.m. ディナー )

## Words and Phrases

| | |
|---|---|
| □本日のおすすめ | today's special |
| □シェフのおすすめ | chef's recommendation |
| □メニュー | menu |
| □開店時間 | open |
| □閉店時間 | close |

## Useful Expressions
### 応用表現

**営業案内**

□月曜から土曜、午前10時から夜11時まで営業しております。
We are open from 10:00 a.m. to 11:00 p.m., from Monday to Saturday.

□ここはチャイナタウンとは少し違った雰囲気です。
We have a slightly different atmosphere than that in Chinatown.

□特別な機会にお使いいただける部屋が5部屋あります。
There are five rooms available for special occasions.

□お客様のお越しをお待ちしております!
We are looking forward to your visit!

**メニュー紹介**

□私たちの料理スタイルは、基本的にフランス料理です。
Our cuisine style is basically French.

□様々なワインも取り揃えております。
A variety of wines will also be available.

□夜は、お酒もお出ししております。
In the evening, liquors are also served.

□全てのメインコースには、新鮮な季節の野菜がついています。

All of our main courses are served with fresh seasonal vegetables.

□経験豊富なシェフが、お客様の目の前で魚介類や国産牛を料理いたします。

We serve excellent Japanese beef as well as seafood, cooked right in front of you by our experienced chefs.

【フランス語のメニュー】

最近ではフランス語で書かれているメニューもよく目にします。
覚えておくと便利でしょう。

| | |
|---|---|
| □アラカルト | à la carte |
| □前菜 | hors d' œuvre |
| □アントレ | entrée |
| □肉料理 | viande |
| □魚料理 | poisson |
| □チーズ | fromage |
| □ワイン | vin |
| □デザート | dessert |
| □飲みもの | boisson |

**You can create your own original goods with your favorite photos!**
**Transform your photos into memorable gifts!**

We offer you several kinds of goods just around your life.
Examples : Postcard, calling card, mouse pad, coaster,
T-shirt, calendar, etc···

☆NEWS☆
Mother's Day Campaign!
Send your mom a cordial gift!!
Click here!

Learn more          Join Now

---

お気に入りの写真でオリジナルグッズを作りましょう！
あなたの写真を記念ギフトにしましょう！

身近なグッズを豊富にご用意しております。
例：ポストカード、テレフォンカード、マウスパッド、コースター、
Tシャツ、カレンダー、等々

☆ニュース☆
母の日キャンペーン実施中！
真心をこめてお母さんにプレゼントを贈りましょう!!
ここをクリックしてください！

詳細を見る          参加する

# Cool Sound Library

## Search

You can search from artist / name of songs, video, DVD.

## Download here

Trial here! (FREE!!!)

Unlimited access to high-speed downloads (members only)

Charge：100 yen for 3 songs / 300 yen for 10 songs

## Burn

Your favorite songs and movies to a CD or DVD!

### JOIN NOW !

---

## クールサウンドライブラリ

### 検索する

アーティスト名や、曲・ビデオ・DVDの名前からの検索が可能です。

### ダウンロードはここから

試　聴！（無料です!!!）

アクセスに制限はなく、高速スピードでのダウンロードが可能（会員のみ）

料金：（3曲 100円、10曲 300円）

### コピーする

お気に入りの曲や映画がそのままCD、DVDへ！

### 今すぐ参加してね！

## Useful Expressions
### 応用表現

**サービス内容**

□オンラインで写真を載せて、その写真を友達や家族と一緒に楽しめます。

You can place your pictures online and share them with your friends and family.

□お試し無料！

Trial for free!

□20枚現像が無料です！

20 FREE prints!

□初回のご注文は、10枚のL版での現像が無料です。

10 FREE model L prints with your very first order!

**ダウンロード**

□ABCソフトのヴァージョンの3.0が利用できます！

ABC software version 3.0 is available now!

□あなたのABCソフトは最新のものではありません。アップグレードが必要です。

Your ABC software is not the latest one. You need to upgrade it.

□音楽ファイルをダウンロードした後、解凍ソフトが必要になります。

You need an expanding software after you download the music file.

□一度ファイルをダウンロードすれば、コンピュータに保存し、何度でも楽しむことができます。

Once you downloaded a file, you can save it in your computer and enjoy forever.

## その他

□無料登録はこちらをクリック！

Click here for free register!

□会員の方のみ、現像やギフトに関して特典があります。

Members-only for special deals on prints and gifts.

□個人情報を登録する必要はありません。

You don't have to register your personal information.

□写真アルバムのシェアは無制限です。

Unlimited photo album sharing.

□デジタル画像をアップロードする必要があります。

You need to upload your digital pictures.

□画質と枚数を選択することができます。

You can choose the quality and quantity of the pictures.

□個性的なギフトを制作することができます。

You can create your own unique gifts.

□25,000枚超のアルバムに無制限にアクセスすることができます。

You can have unlimited access to more than 25,000 albums.

□莫大なストリーミング音楽のライブラリを提供しています。

We offer you a huge library of streaming music.

□好きなミュージシャンのライブ映像を、自宅でいつでも見ることができます。

You can watch live scenes of your favorite musician at home whenever you like.

□セキュリティ関連は、こちらをクリックしてご確認ください。

Please click and check here about security concerns.

# 4．オンライン購入

## ①トップページ

Welcome to ABC Online Store!  Enjoy shopping with us!

　◇Already a customer?  Sign in!

　◇New Customer?  Click here!
　Once you've registered, you'll be able to experience special features!
　A history of what you've purchased will be available to you anytime.

ABCオンラインストアにようこそ！当サイトでのお買い物をお楽しみください！

　◇既存のお客様ですか？サインインしてください！

　◇新しいお客様ですか？こちらをクリックしてください！
　ご登録いただくと、特典があります！
　いつでも購入履歴をご覧いただけます。

## Words and Phrases

| | |
|---|---|
| □サインインする | sign in |
| □登録する | register |
| □暗証番号 | personal identification number (=pin) |
| □広告 | advertisement（＝ad） |
| □ユーザーの感想 | user review |
| □日本でのみ有効です | only available in Japan |

## Useful Expressions
### 応用表現

**会員の人に**

□サインインしますか。
Would you like to sign in?

□既存のお客様ですか。
Returning customer?

□パスワードをお忘れですか？こちらをクリックしてください。
Forgot your password? Click here.

□最近の注文を見る。
Track your recent order.

**会員登録**

□まだ登録されていませんか。
Not registered yet?

□オンラインアカウントをつくるには、要求されたすべての情報を記入してください。

Please fill out all requested information to create an online account.

☐1,000円お得（節約）！
Save ¥1,000!

☐5月いっぱいは、弊社オリジナルコーヒーメーカーが通常4,000円のところ、なんと3,500円！
During the whole month of May, our original coffee maker is only ¥3,500 instead of ¥4,000!

☐このプロモーションは、次の製品が対象になります。
This promotion is for the following products:

☐7月5日まで、ABCオンラインストアで6,000円より多くご注文いただいた場合は、送料無料！
Now through July 5th, get free shipping on orders over ¥6,000 from ABC online store.

☐5,000円以上お買い上げで、送料無料！
Free shipping on your purchase of ¥5,000 or more!

☐包装、税金、送料は、対象金額には計算されません。
Packaging, taxes, and shipping and handling do not count toward the qualifying amount.

☐セール品は、クーポン券ご利用の対象外となります。
Sale merchandise is not valid for coupons.

☐お忘れなく！母の日は5月11日！
Don't forget! Mother's day is May 11th!

その他

☐この情報は、2003年9月1日現在のものです。
This information is current as of September 1st, 2003.

□このページを友人に送る（リンクが貼られている場合）

Send this page to a friend

□カタログをご希望の方は、こちらをクリックしてください。

To request a catalog, click here.

□メーリングリストへの参加をご希望の方は、Eメールアドレスを入力してください。

Enter your e-mail address to join our mailing list.

□ABC.Comは現在閉店しています。

ABC. Com is currently closed.

□左のメニューバーで、必要な情報を探してください。

Use the menu bar on the left to find the information you need.

□弊社は、海外のお客様に次のショッピングオプションをご提供しております。

We offer our international customers the following shopping options:

---

**【オンライン購入によく見られる項目・表現】**

| | |
|---|---|
| □買物カゴを見る | View Cart |
| □新しい注文 | New Order |
| □注文状況 | Order Status |
| □商品 | Products |
| □カタログ | Catalog |
| □IDとパスワード | ID & Password |
| □検索する | Search |
| □検索をしぼる | Narrow Your Search |
| □予定配達日を見る | See Your Estimated Delivery Date |
| □カスタマーサービス | Customer Service |
| □セキュリティとプライバシー | Security and Privacy |
| □取引条件 | Terms and Conditions |
| □写真があります | have a photo |
| □ご注文の品を確認する | confirm your items ordered |
| □Eメール通知 | E-mail Notification |

②注　文

Stretch Satin Pants
¥8,900
original price ¥12,800
Detail

Denim Skirt
¥5,500

Detail

Black Slingback
¥13,000

Detail

ストレッチサテンパンツ
¥8,900
定価¥12,800
詳細

デニムスカート
¥5,500

詳細

黒のバックストラップ靴
¥13,000

詳細

| | |
|---|---|
| □注文する | order／place an order |
| □注文を取り消す | cancel an order |
| □買物カゴ、ショッピングカート | shopping cart |
| □買物カゴの中を見る | view shopping cart |
| □買物カゴに加える | add to shopping cart |
| □買物カゴから削除する | remove from shopping cart |
| □品目 | item |
| □単価 | unit price |
| □定価 | list price／original price |
| □特別価格 | special price／special value |
| □数量 | quantity |
| □値引き | discount／reduction |
| □消費税 | tax |
| □小計 | subtotal |
| □合計 | total |
| □精算する | check out |
| □配送先 | shipping address |
| □請求先 | billing address |
| □節約する | save |
| □お試しセット | trial set |
| □商品券 | gift certificate |
| □引き換える | redeem |
| □商品券を商品に換える | redeem a gift certificate |
| □新着商品 | new arrivals |
| □荷物を受け取る | receive a package |
| □営業日 | business day |
| □確認 | confirmation |
| □買物を続ける | continue shopping |
| □完了する | complete |
| □価格帯 | price range |

# Useful Expressions
## 応用表現

### 商品の説明

□大きい画像を見るには、ここをクリック。

Click here to see a large image.

□別の色を見る。

View another color.

□サイズによってはご提供していない色もございます。

All colors may not be available in all sizes.

□こちらの黒い革のベルトもおすすめです。

We also suggest this black leather belt.

＊本章3．製品・サービス案内のページも参照してください。

### 注文の状況

□カゴには、現在何も入っていません。

Your shopping cart is currently empty.

□カゴには商品がありません。

There are no items in your cart.

□現在、買物カゴに3品目入っています。

You currently have three items in your cart.

□買物カゴの中の品物：1つ

Items in shopping cart:1

□ご注文の詳細が閲覧できます。

You can view details of your order.

### 注文を受け付ける

□ご注文は処理されました。

Your order has been processed.

□支払方法が認可され次第、製造に入ります。

Your order will go into production upon authorization of your method of payment.

□午後2時以降にいただいたご注文は、翌営業日の処理となります。

Orders received after 2:00 p.m. will be processed the next business day.

□24時間以内に、注文確認メールをお送りします。ご注文の詳細を再確認いただき、このメールを保存してください。

We'll send you the order confirmation by e-mail within 24 hours. Please review your order details and save the e-mail.

□注文確認メールには、あなたの顧客番号と注文番号が記載されています。

The order confirmation e-mail contains your customer number and your order number.

## 注文を取り消す

□商品を取り消すには、「キャンセル」ボタンをクリックしてください。

To delete an item, please click on the "cancel" button.

## 注文番号

□注文番号は8桁です。

Your order number is eight digits long.

□注文番号は、注文確認メールの中に記載されています。

Your order number will be in your order confirmation e-mail.

## 配達日時

□カナダへの配達日数は、5～10営業日です。

Delivery time to Canada is 5-10 business days.

□ご注文いただく際に、選択された発送オプションに基づいて、発送および配達日を見積もります。

When you place an order, we will estimate shipping and delivery dates for you, based on the shipping options you choose.

□発送予定日は注文書に表示されます。

Shipping date estimates will appear in the order form.

□ご注文されますと、注文確認メールで発送および配達予定日をご覧いただけます。

Once you've placed your order, you will be able to see both shipping and delivery date estimates in the order confirmation e-mail.

□配達日をご指定いただけます。

You can specify the delivery date.

□ご注文品が発送されたら、出荷状況をEメールにて通知いたします。

Once your order has been shipped, we will notify you via e-mail of the shipment status.

□送料は、選択された配送方法によります。

Shipping costs depend upon the shipping methods you choose.

□お選びになった配送方法により、配達日が決定されます。

The shipping method you choose determines your order's arrival date.

□送料は重量基準となっていますので、ご注意ください。

Please note that the shipping rates are weight-based.

□ほとんどの注文品は、祝日、週末を除き、2〜3営業日内に出荷されます。

Most orders are shipped within 2-3 business days, not including holidays or weekends.

□商品の在庫がある場合は、2〜3日で倉庫から発送されます。

If the merchandise is in stock, your order should leave our warehouse in 2-3 days.

□商品が注文品の場合は、もう7〜10日かかります。

If the merchandise is on backorder, it may take an additional 7-10 days.

□通常、ご注文後1〜3営業日以内に出荷いたします。

Usually, your order is shipped within 1-3 business days after your order.

□5月10日に確実に届けるには、普通便なら5月1日午後3時まで、特急便なら5月5日正午までにご注文ください。

To ensure a May 10th delivery, orders must be placed by 3:00 p.m. May 1st for standard shipping or by noon May 5th for express shipping.

□ご注文の品が出荷されたら、Eメールをお送りすることもできます。

We can also send you an e-mail when your order has shipped.

□ご注文品の出荷後に、荷物の状況についての情報をもっとご覧いただけます。

After your order ships, you will see more information about the status of your packages.

□注文品が出荷されたらEメールを受け取る。

Receive an e-mail when your order ships.

## 商品券

□商品券は譲渡できません。

Gift certificates are non-transferable.

□弊社の商品券は、1,000円から10,000円の間でご利用いただけます。

Our gift certificates are available for any amount between ¥1,000 and ¥10,000.

□一度に5枚まで商品券を引き換えられます。

You can redeem up to five gift certificates at a time.

□商品券の損失につきましては、責任を負いかねます。

We aren't responsible for lost gift certificates.

□シリアル番号がある商品券のみ有効です。

A valid gift certificate must have a serial number.

□商品券を現金とお引き換えすることはできません。

This gift certificate has no cash value.

□商品券の価格が合計金額を超えている場合は、現金の返金はできません。

If the value of your gift certificate exceeds the total amount, no cash refund will be made.

□商品券は、ABCストア全店でお引き換えいただけます。

Gift certificates can be redeemed at any ABC store.

## 質 問

□さらに質問がございましたら、弊社のカスタマーサポートサイトを閲覧してください。

If you have additional questions, please visit our customer support web site.

□よくあるご質問に対する回答が分かります。

You can get answers to common questions.

□他の問題に関しては、ご連絡ください。

For other issues, please contact us.

## その他

□贈り物は、ギフトボックスに入れてリボンをおかけします。料金は1パッケージにつき、3ドルとなっております。

We'll wrap your gift in our gift box with a ribbon. The charge is just $3 per package.

□注文ページに戻るには、ブラウザの一番上にある「戻る」ボタンをクリックしてください。

To return to the order page, click on the "BACK" button at the top of the browser.

□ABCをお選びいただき、ありがとうございます。

Thank you for choosing ABC.

# ③支払方法・条件

## Payment Method

We accept the following methods of payment for online orders:
- VISA
- MasterCard
- American Express
- Gift Card

Currently, debit cards are not allowed.

## 支払方法

オンライン注文では、次の支払方法を受け付けております。
- ビザ
- マスターカード
- アメリカンエキスプレス
- ギフトカード

現在、デビッドカードはお使いになれません。

## Words and Phrases

| | |
|---|---|
| □支払い | payment |
| □支払方法 | payment method |
| □支払方法の選択肢 | payment options |
| □送料 | shipping and handling fee |
| □代金引換え払い | cash on delivery (=C. O. D) |

Ⅲ ホームページでよく使う表現

# Useful Expressions
## 応用表現

### 支払条件・方法

□支払いは、次の2つのいずれかの方法でお願いします。
Payment shall be made in either of the following two ways:

□小切手も受け付けております。
We also accept checks.

□請求書を閲覧できます。
You can view your invoice.

□送料など、さらなる情報を見たい方は、こちらをクリックしてください。
Click here for more information, including shipping rates.

□商品発送時に、クレジットカードに請求いたします。
Your credit card will be charged when your order is shipped.

### 商品の料金・送料

□送料と税金が注文代金に加算されます。
Shipping and tax may be added to your order.

□2,500円以上のご注文は送料無料！
Now free shipping on orders of ¥2,500 or more!

□全品、送料無料！
Free shipping on everything!

□速達をお選びの方は、追加料金がかかります。
If you choose rush shipping, additional charges may apply.

□送料は、精算する際に計算されます。
The shipping charges are calculated when you check out.

## Order Tracking

Our order tracking system shows the status of an order anytime. In order to track your order, you will need both your order number and the e-mail address used to place the order.

Email Address: [＿＿＿＿＿＿＿＿]
Order Number: [＿＿＿＿＿＿＿＿]

[ Track ]

## 注文の追跡

当注文追跡システムでは、いつでも注文の状態をご覧いただけます。ご注文品を追跡するには、注文番号と、ご注文の際にご使用になったＥメールアドレスが必要になります。

Ｅメールアドレス： [＿＿＿＿＿＿＿＿]
注文番号　　　　： [＿＿＿＿＿＿＿＿]

[ 追跡 ]

| | |
|---|---|
| □注文状況 | order status |
| □注文番号 | purchase order number（=P. O. No.) |
| □出荷予定日 | estimated shipping date |
| □到着予定日 | estimated arrival date |
| □配送情報 | shipping information |
| □追跡する | track |

## Useful Expressions
### 応用表現

**注文品の追跡**

□情報を入力して、特定のウェブでの注文を追跡できます。

You may track a specific web order by entering the information.

□注文番号により注文状況が追跡できます。

The order number allows you to track your order's status.

□一度に2件以上のご注文状況を確認したい方は、顧客番号に関連した全注文をご覧いただけます。

If you'd like to check on the status of more than one order at a time, you can view all your orders associated with a customer number.

□注文番号またはお客様番号であなたのご注文が探せます。

You can find your order by order number or customer number.

□上記リストに注文されたものが入っていないときには、こちらに注文番号を入力して注文状況を確認してください。

If you don't see your order in the above list, enter your order No. here to check on its status.

□注文番号で注文を並べ替えることができます。

You can sort your orders by order number.

# ⑤返品規約

**Our Returns Policy**

Need to return an item?
Returns are easy!

We cannot accept returns of certain items, including:
- Any item that is returned more than 14 days after delivery.
- Any CD that has been opened.

Our return address is:
1-2-3, Nishi-Shinjuku, Shinjuku-ku, Tokyo

返品規約

返品しますか？
返品は簡単です！

次の商品は返品を受け付けておりません：
- 配達後14日を過ぎて返品された商品
- 開封済みのＣＤ

返品先：
東京都新宿区西新宿１－２－３

Ⅲ　ホームページでよく使う表現

## Words and Phrases

| | |
|---|---|
| ☐返品規約 | return policy |
| ☐返品する | return |
| ☐交換する | exchange |
| ☐返金 | refund |
| ☐荷物の中に入っている伝票、納品書 | packing slip |

## Useful Expressions
### 応用表現

返品・交換

☐簡単に返品、交換！

Easy returns and exchanges!

☐配達から15日以内であれば、どんな品物でも返品を受け付け、全額返金いたします。

You may return all items within 15 days of delivery for a full refund.

☐弊社カタログからお買い上げいただいた全商品の返品を受け付けております。

We accept returns on all merchandise purchased from our catalog.

☐返金規約、その他に関しては、こちらをクリックしてください。

Please click here for our refund policy and more.

☐返品規約をご覧ください。

Please review the return policy.

☐破損、欠陥、品違いの場合は、弊社が返品送料負担いたします。

If you received a damaged, defective, or incorrect item, we'll pay the return shipping cost.

☐送料は返金できませんので、ご了承ください。

Please note, shipping and handling charges are non-refundable.

266

□返品された場合は、商品券も返却いたします。

For return items, gift certificates must be returned as well.

【Price Adjustmentsとは…】
日本では見られませんが、アメリカでは店頭購入の場合（オンライン購入での適用例もある）、"Price Adjustments（価格調整）"が多く行われています。たとえば、靴を100ドルで購入した翌日、同じ店に行ってみたらセールで80ドルになっていた場合、購入者は、差額の20ドルを返金してもらえます。店によって "Price Adjustments" が適用される日数が決められています。

【位置を表す表現】

| | |
|---|---|
| ～の上の | on the top of ～ |
| ～の下の | at the bottom of ～ |
| 下の | below |
| ～の隣の | next to ～ |
| ～の上の | above ～ |
| | |
| ～以上 | ～ and more |
| ～以下 | ～ and less |
| ～より上の | over ～ |
| ～未満 | under ～ |

# 5. FAQs（よくある質問）

You can get answers to common questions.
For other issues, please contact us.

● How do I cancel an order?
● How do I download a sample software?
● What is the return policy?
● I placed an order over the web, but I made a mistake. How can I correct it?

・
・
・

よくある質問へのお答えが分かります。
その他の質問に関しては、ご連絡ください。

● どうやって注文をキャンセルするの？
● サンプルソフトウェアはどうやってダウンロードするの？
● 返品規約って何？
● ウェブ上で注文したが、間違えた。どうやって訂正するの？

・
・
・

## Words and Phrases

| | |
|---|---|
| □よく聞かれる質問 | frequently asked question |
| □よくある質問 | common question |
| □一般的な質問 | general question |
| □注文に関するヘルプ | order assistance |
| □ダウンロードに関するヘルプ | download assistance |
| □技術サポート | technical support |

## Useful Expressions
### 応用表現

□Q：ABCストアでどうやって注文するのですか。

How can I order on ABC store?

A：オンライン、電話、ファックス、Eメールと、便利な4種類の注文方法があります。

We offer four convenient ways of ordering: Online, By Phone, By Fax or By E-mail.

□Q：今日注文したら、品物はいつ出荷されますか。

If I place my order today, when will the order be shipped?

A：午後3時（東部標準時間）までにいただいたご注文はすべて、1営業日内に発送いたします。営業日は、休日を除く月曜日から金曜日となっております。

All orders received by 3:00 p.m. EST will be shipped within one business day. Business days are Monday through Friday, excluding holidays.

□Q：卸売り価格は提供されていますか。

Do you offer wholesale pricing?

A：提供しております。詳しくは、123-456-789までお電話ください。

Yes, we offer wholesale pricing. Please call 123-456-789 for more information.

□Q：どんな支払方法がありますか？
   What forms of payment are accepted?

 A：次の方法があります。
   - Aカード
   - Bカード
   - ギフトカード
   We accept the following:
   - A card
   - B card
   - gift card

□Q：どんなクレジットカードが使えますか。
   What credit cards do you accept?

 A：A、B、Cなどの主要なクレジットカードはすべてお使いになれます。
   We accept all major credit cards: A, B, and C.

□Q：インターネット上でクレジットカードを使用しても安全ですか？
   Is it safe to use my credit card over the Internet?

 A：はい。弊社はSSL技術を使用し、クレジットカード情報が弊社に送られる
   際の安全を確保しています。
   Yes. We use SSL technology to protect the security of your credit
   card information as it is transmitted to us.

□Q：海外に発送できますか？
   Do you ship to international addresses?

 A：現在、海外からのご注文はお請けしておりません
   At this time, we are unable to accept international orders.

□Q：どうして注文確認メールが届かないのでしょう？
   Why didn't I receive an order confirmation e-mail?

A：間違ったEメールアドレスが入力された可能性があります。弊社カスタマーサービス03-123-4567までお電話ください。

An incorrect e-mail address may have been entered.  Please call our customer service at 03-123-4567.

☐Q：どうして発送通知が届かないのでしょう？

Why didn't I receive a shipping notification?

A：間違ったEメールアドレスが入力された可能性があります。注文確認番号をご用意のうえ、弊社カスタマーサービス03-123-4567までお電話ください。ご注文品の状況をご確認いたします。

An incorrect e-mail address may have been entered. Please call our customer service at 03-123-4567 with your order confirmation number, and we will confirm your order status.

☐Q：注文をキャンセルするにはどうすればよいでしょうか。

How do I cancel an order?

A：ABC.comでのご注文をキャンセルまたは変更したい場合は、できるだけ早く〈03-1234-5678〉までお電話ください。発送工程に入ってしまうと、キャンセルも変更もできかねます。

If you would like to cancel or change your order with ABC.com, please call us at 03-1234-5678 as soon as possible.  We cannot cancel or change an order once it has entered the shipping process.

☐Q：パスワードを忘れました。どうすればいいですか。

I forgot my password.  What should I do?

A：パスワードを忘れた場合は、トップページにある「Forgot Your Password?」リンクをクリックしてください。

If you forget your password, click on the "Forgot Your Password?" link on the top page.

☐Q：送料はどうなっていますか。

What's the shipping charge?

A：送料は、製品の重量によります。

The shipping charge is based on the weight of the product.

□Q：アップグレード商品を購入できる？

Am I eligible to purchase an upgrade?

A：購入したい製品の前ヴァージョンの登録ユーザであれば、現ヴァージョンを特別アップグレード価格でご購入いただけます。

If you are a registered user of a previous version of the same product that you want to purchase, you are eligible to purchase the current version at a special upgrade price.

□Q：ダウンロードにどのくらい時間がかかる？

How long is my download going to take?

A：ダウンロードの時間はあくまでも概算であり、システム、接続速度によります。

Download times are just an estimate and depend on your system and the speed of your connection.

# 6．採用情報

ABC Corporation has a variety of career opportunities.
If you would like to learn more about working at ABC Corporation,
please e-mail your resume with a cover letter to: career@abc.com

Thank you for your interest.

ABC社にはいろいろな採用の機会がございます。
ABC社での勤務についてさらに知りたい場合は、履歴書にカバーレターをつけて、career@abc.com までEメールで送信してください。

ご関心をお寄せいただきありがとうございます。

## Words and Phrases

| | |
|---|---|
| □経歴 | career |
| □履歴書 | resume |
| □申請書 | application form |
| □申し込む | apply |
| □職種 | position |
| □職務経歴 | business background |
| □経験 | experience |
| □採用条件 | hiring requirements／ |
| | conditions of employment |
| □面接 | interview |
| □リクルートイベント | recruiting event |
| □学生向け就職フェア | student career fairs |

| | |
|---|---|
| □応募方法 | how to apply |
| □現場実習 | on-the-job training |
| □社外実習 | off-the-job training |
| □提出する | submit |
| □募集中の仕事を調べる | explore available jobs |

## Useful Expressions
## 応用表現

**募集内容**

□募集している職種を下から検索できます。
You can search through our open positions below.

□現在、次の職種が採用可能です。
The following positions are available at this time:

□ABC社は、ウェブデザイナー、ウェブ開発者、ソフトウェア開発エンジニアのような、多分野における熟練者を求めています。
ABC Corporation is looking for individuals proficient in many areas including:
Web Designer, Web Developer, Software Development Engineer.

□新宿にあるABCは、店長経験者を求めています。
ABC, located in Shinjuku, needs an experienced store manager.

□このポストは、ABCストアの円滑かつ能率的な運営を行う責任があります。
The position is responsible for the smooth and efficient operation of an ABC store.

□仕事の分野をクリックしてください。
Click on a job category.

□申し込みたい仕事をクリックしてください。
Click on the job you want to apply for.

□あなたの適性と雇用ニーズが合えば、雇用部門の者より連絡させていただきます。

If there's a match with your qualifications and our employment needs, you will be contacted by a member of the recruiting department.

### 応募資格

□カスタマーサービスでの経験が好ましい。

Experience in customer service is preferred.

□学士号が必要です。また、経営学修士号があれば好ましいです。

A bachelor's degree is required, and an M.B.A. is preferred.

□最低でも2年間のカスタマーサービスでの経験があること。

At least two years customer service experience.

□採用、従業員のスケジュール管理、在庫管理を含む、小売管理経験が1〜2年あること。

1-2 years of work experience within retail management including:

−Recruitment
−Employee scheduling
−Inventory control

### 雇用条件

□週5日勤務。

Five-day work week.

□ABC社は、他社に負けない給与とすばらしい福利厚生を提供します。

ABC Corporation offers competitive compensation and outstanding benefits.

□ほとんどの特権が勤務初日から有効になります。

Most benefits are active on the first day of employment.

□福利厚生には20日間の有給休暇、当社商品の50%オフなどが含まれます。

Benefits include 20 paid holidays, 50% discount on our products and more!

□履歴書をお送りください。

Please send us your resume.

□魅力的な履歴書作成には、弊社の履歴書作成ツールをご利用ください。

Use our resume builder to create an attractive resume.

□左のアイコンをクリックして、Word形式の応募用紙をダウンロードしてください。

Click on the icon to the left to download the application form in Word format.

□ここをクリックして、Word形式の応募用紙の記入例をご覧ください。

Please click here to see an example of a completed application form in Word format.

□オンライン履歴書作成ツールを使用して、履歴書とカバーレターを提出してください。

Please submit your resume and cover letter using the online resume builder.

## その他

□ABC社への就職に関心をお寄せいただき、ありがとうございます。

Thank you for your interest in employment with ABC Corporation.

□弊社担当者と面会するこの機会をお見逃しなく！

Take advantage of this great opportunity to meet our representative!

□あなたの技能と希望に関する情報をください。当社であなたに適した仕事が分かります。

Give us a little information regarding your skills and desires, and we'll find the perfect job for you at our company.

□現在、採用は行っておりません。

Currently there are no job openings.

# 7．資料請求

Please complete the following form to receive our catalog.

Title：
First Name：
Last Name：
Address：
City：
State：
Country：
Zip Code：
Phone：
Fax：
E-mail Address：
Company Name：
Position：

| Send | | Reset |

カタログが欲しい方は、次のフォームに記入してください。

敬称：

名前：

姓：

住所：

都市名：

州名：

国名：

郵便番号：

電話：

ファックス：

Eメールアドレス：

会社名：

役職：

| 送　信 | | リセット |
|---|---|---|

## Words and Phrases

| □資料請求 | information request |
|---|---|
| □記入する | complete／fill in／fill out |
| □送信 | send |
| □リセット | reset |
| □無料カタログ | free catalog |
| □無料サンプル | free sample |

## Useful Expressions
### 応用表現

☐次のフォームに記入してください。
Please complete the following form.

☐下のフォームに記入してください。
Please fill out the form below.

☐Eメールで情報を送信してください。
Please send your information by e-mail.

☐Eメールアドレスは必ず入力してください。
Please make sure to enter your e-mail address.

☐資料を郵送にて受け取りたい方は、次のフォームに記入してください。
To receive information by postal mail, please complete the following form.

☐ABCからの無料カタログを受け取るには、下のフォームに記入してください。
To receive a free catalog from ABC, please fill out the form below.

☐2～3週間でカタログをお届けします。
You will receive a catalog in a few weeks.

☐カタログは、日本とアメリカの住所にのみお送りします。
We are able to send our catalog to addresses in Japan and the U.S. only.

☐分からなければ、空欄にしておいてください。
Leave blank if unsure.

**【資料請求フォームの項目】**

- □敬称：title
- □名前：last name
- □姓：first name
- □住所：address
- □都市名：city
- □州名：state
- □国名：country
- □郵便番号：zip code
- □電話：phone
- □ファックス：fax
- □メールアドレス：e-mail address
- □会社名：company name
- □役職：position
- □年齢：age
- □送付先住所：shipping address

# 8．問い合わせ

会社への問い合わせ先を簡潔にまとめます。住所、電話、ファックス、Ｅメール等を記載します。

---

**Contact Us:**

If you've got questions, comments or suggestions, feel free to contact us anytime, before or after a purchase.

Tel: +81-3-1234-5678
Fax: +81-3-1234-5679
E-mail: info@abc.com
Mailing address: 1-2-3, Nishi-Shinjuku
　　　　　　　　　Shinjuku-ku, 123-4567, Tokyo

---

お問い合わせ：

質問、ご意見、ご提案がございましたら、ご購入前、後にかかわらず、お気軽にお問い合わせください。

電話番号： +81-3-1234-5678
ファックス番号： +81-3-1234-5679
Ｅメール: info@abc.com
郵送先: 〒123-4567
　　　東京都新宿区西新宿１－２－３

## Words and Phrases

□お問い合わせください（問い合わせページのタイトル）　　contact us

□問い合わせ情報　　　　　　　　　contact information

□問い合わせ　　　　　　　　　　　inquiry

□カスタマーサービスセンター　　　customer service center

□技術サポート　　　　　　　　　　technical support

□お気軽に〜してください　　　　　feel free to 〜

## Useful Expressions

### 応用表現

**問い合わせ先の案内**

□さらにABC社の情報が欲しい場合は、以下の宛先にご連絡ください。

For additional information about ABC company, please contact us at the following address:

□以下の製品に関するご質問は、kobayashi@abc.com 宛にお願いします。

For questions related to the following products, contact us at kobayashi@abc.com

□ウェブマスターにご連絡ください。

Please contact our webmaster.

□さらに情報がほしい方は、（012）345-6789にお電話していただくか、info@abc.comまでEメールでご連絡ください。

For more information, call us at (012)345-6789, or e-mail us at info@abc.com

□ご購入前にご質問がございましたら、いつでもお気軽にEメールにてお問い合わせください。

If you have questions before your purchase, please feel free to contact us anytime by e-mail.

□製品に関する問い合わせ、価格のご確認、ご注文には、ABC営業担当者がいつ
でも対応いたします。

Whenever you want to inquire about products, check prices or place
an order, ABC sales representatives are always standing by.

□電話やファックスでもお問い合わせいただけます。

You can also contact us by phone or fax.

□技術サポートは、月曜から金曜の、太平洋時間で午前6時から午後5時までと
なっております。

Technical support is available from 6:00 a.m. to 5:00 p.m. Pacific
time, Monday through Friday.

□ハードウェア／ソフトウェアの注文、ハードウェアのメンテナンスに関しては、
こちらの番号におかけください。

You may call this number concerning questions on hardware /
software orders and hardware maintenance.

□インストールまたは製品の使用に関しての問題の解決方法を見つけるには、こ
ちらをクリックしてください。

Click here to find answers to problems regarding installing or using
our products.

□さらに情報がほしい方は、こちらをクリックしてください。

Click here for more information.

□もしあなたの質問がコンサルティングサービスに関するものであれば、以下の
リンクをご利用ください。

If your question is about our consulting service, please use the link
below.

## 連絡前の注意事項

□ご連絡いただく前に、下のリンクリストに目を通してください。

Please take a look at our list of links below before you contact us.

□ウェブでご質問の回答をご提供しているかもしれません。

We may already provide the answer to your question on the web.

□お問い合わせの前にFAQsをご覧ください。

Please read our FAQs before contacting us.

## 意見などを求める

□ご質問、ご意見、ご提案をお送りください。

Please send us your questions, comments and suggestions.

□ウェブサイトのバグの報告、サイトに関するフィードバック、コメントをぜひ
お送りください。

Report a web site bug, send feedback about our web site or send
comments to us.

# 9. リンクボタン

インターネットでよく使われているリンクボタンをまとめました。

| | |
|---|---|
| □クリックする | click |
| □ここをクリックする | click here |
| □閲覧する | browse |
| □閲覧する | view |
| □送信する | send |
| □リセットする | reset |
| □検索する | search |
| □実行する | go |
| □こちらからスタートする | start here |
| □ログインする | log in |
| □ログアウトする | log out |
| □次へ | next |
| □～に戻る | back to ～／return to ～ |
| □ダウンロードする | download |
| □このページを印刷する | print this page |
| □トップページ（ホームページ）へ | back to top／home／top page／top of page |
| □閉じる | close |
| □提出する | submit |
| □検索オプション | advanced search |
| □オンラインデモを閲覧する | view online demonstration |
| □イベント予定 | upcoming events |
| □ABCのデータについてもっと知る | learn more about ABC's data |

# IV

## すぐに役立つ会社の資料

# 1．会社の書類

| | |
|---|---|
| ☐ 会社案内 | a company brochure |
| ☐ 製品カタログ | a product catalog |
| ☐ 価格表 | a price list |
| ☐ 見積書 | a quote／quotation／estimate |
| ☐ 注文書 | an order sheet／an order form／ |
| | a purchase order sheet |
| ☐ 注文請書 | an order acknowledgement |
| ☐ 注文確認書 | an order confirmation |
| ☐ 契約書 | a contract |
| ☐ 通知書 | a notification |
| ☐ 納品書 | a statement of delivery |
| ☐ 受領書 | an acknowledgement |
| ☐ 領収書 | a receipt |
| ☐ 送り状・請求書 | an invoice |
| ☐ 請求書 | a bill |
| ☐ 督促状 | a reminder |
| ☐ 信用状 | a letter of credit（L/C） |
| ☐ 保証状 | a letter of guarantee （L/G） |
| ☐ 紹介状 | a letter of reference |
| ☐ 推薦状 | a letter of recommendation |
| ☐ 船積書類 | shipping documents |
| ☐ 船荷証券 | bill of lading（B/L） |
| ☐ 検査証明書 | a certificate of inspection |
| ☐ 名刺 | a business card |
| ☐ 書類 | a document／a paper |
| ☐ 資料 | data／materials |
| ☐ 議事録 | minutes |
| ☐ メモ・覚書 | a memo |

| | |
|---|---|
| □ 報告書 | a report |
| □ 年次報告書 | an annual report |
| □ 損益計算書 | a profit and loss statement |
| □ タイムカード | a time card |
| □ 履歴書 | a resume |

# 2. 数　字

数 <Number>

種類　基数　a cardinal number

　　　序数　an ordinal number

　　　分数　a fraction

　　　少数　a decimal

　　　偶数　an even number ⇔ 奇数　an uneven number（an odd number）


単位 <Unit>

| | |
|---|---|
| ～度（° ） | degree |
| 摂氏（℃） | centigrade ⇔ 華氏（°Ｆ）fahrenheit |
| グラム（g） | gram |
| キログラム（kg） | kilogram |
| トン（t） | ton |
| ポンド（lb） | pound |
| センチメートル（cm） | centimeter |
| メートル（m） | meter |
| マイル（mile） | mile |
| パーセント（%） | percent |
| 回転速度：回毎分（rpm） | revolution per minute |
| 　　　　　時速（km／h） | kilometer per hour |
| その他：ダース | dozen = 12 |
| 　　　　半ダース | half dozen = 6 |
| | ※ score = 20 |

# 3. 組織を表す単語一覧

会社によって組織の規模が違いますので、組織の大きさにより、適切な単語を選択する必要があります。

| | |
|---|---|
| 本社 | Head Office／Headquarters |
| 支社・支店 | Branch Office |
| 営業所 | Sales Branch（Office） |
| 工場 | Factory／Plant |
| 研究所 | Laboratory |
| 本部・事業本部 | Division（Div.） |
| 部 | Department（Dept.） |
| 室 | Office |
| 課 | Section（Sect.） |
| 班 | Team / Group |
| ～係・～担当 | in charge of ～ |
| | （名刺にはin charge ofを付ける必要はない） |
| 第1～ | First ～ |
| 第2～ | Second ～ |
| 第3～ | Third ～ |

例）

| | |
|---|---|
| 第1営業部 | First Sales Dept. |
| 第2営業部 | Second Sales Dept. |
| 第3営業部 | Third Sales Dept. |

＊様々な部署名＊（五十音順）

部署名も会社によっては業務内容が異なりますので、実際の業務内容を表す部署名を付けましょう。以下は一例として挙げます。

| | |
|---|---|
| 営業 | Sales |
| 営業管理 | Sales Administration |
| 営業企画 | Marketing Strategy |

| | |
|---|---|
| 海外営業 | Overseas Sales |
| 海外事業 | Overseas Business |
| 外注 | Subcontracting |
| 監査 | Audit |
| 企画 | Planning／Corporate Planning |
| 機材 | Machinery |
| 技術 | Technical／Engineering |
| 技術開発 | Technology Development |
| 教育研修 | Education and Training |
| 経営企画 | Strategic Planning |
| 経理 | Accounting／General Accounting |
| 研究開発 | Research and Development |
| 検査 | Inspection |
| 厚生 | Welfare |
| 購買 | Purchase |
| 広報 | Public Relations |
| 広報宣伝 | Advertising and Information |
| 国内事業 | Domestic Business |
| サービス | Service |
| 財務 | Finance |
| 資材 | Material |
| 市場開発 | Marketing |
| 渉外 | Liaison |
| 商品企画 | Product Development |
| 人材開発 | Human Resources Development |
| 人事 | Human Resource／Personnel |
| 生産管理 | Production Control |
| 生産技術 | Production Engineering／Production Technology |
| 製造 | Production／Manufacturing |
| 施工／工事 | Construction |
| 設計 | Design |

| | |
|---|---|
| 宣伝 | Advertising and Sales Promotion |
| 総務 | General Affairs |
| 通信 | Communications |
| 電算（室） | Computer（Room） |
| 販売促進 | Sales Promotion |
| 秘書（室） | Secretaries' Office／Secretariat |
| 品質管理 | Quality Control |
| 品質保証 | Quality Assurance |
| 輸出 | Export |
| 輸送 | Traffic |
| 輸入 | Import |
| 労務 | Labor／Labor Relations |

# 4．役職を表す単語一覧

| | |
|---|---|
| 最高経営責任者 | CEO = Chief Executive Officer |
| 最高財務責任者 | CFO = Chief Financial Officer |
| 代表取締役 | Representative Director |
| 社長 | President |
| 副社長 | Executive Vice President |
| 取締役 | Director |

＊取締役会は、"the board of director"といいます。

| | |
|---|---|
| 専務取締役 | Senior Managing Director |
| 常務取締役 | Managing Director |
| 相談役 | Senior Adviser |
| 顧問 | (corporate) Adviser |
| 監査役 | Auditor |

＊"General Manager, ～ Dept." のように後ろに部門名をつけます。(以下
のものもすべて同様)

| | |
|---|---|
| 部長 | General Manager |
| 次長、副～ | Deputy Manager |
| 課長 | Manager |
| 係長 | Section Chief |
| 主任 | Senior Staff |
| ～付 | Assistant to ～ |
| 代理 | Deputy |
| 　例) 営業部長代理 | Deputy Manager, Sales Dept. |
| 補佐 | Assistant ～, 部署 |
| 代行 | Acting ～, 部署 |
| 秘書 | Secretary |
| 　例) ～付秘書 | Secretary to ～ |
| 支店長・所長 | General Manager／～ Branch Office |
| 工場長 | General Manager／～ Works |

著者略歴

## 株式会社ディー・オー・エム・フロンティア

ISOコンサルティングを中心とし、IT（情報技術）を活用したサービス提供を目的として、2001年に株式会社ディー・オー・エムより独立、新会社として発足。ISO9001／14001コンサルティングの経験・ノウハウを活かし、高品質・低価格のコンサルティング方式（ISO9001 e-Consulting、ISO14001 e-Consulting）を開発し、好評を得ている。また、情報セキュリティ関連コンサルティング、CSR（企業の社会的責任）コンサルティング、各種翻訳業務、文書の電子管理サービス、PLコンサルティング、企業内研修なども提供している。

## 味園真紀（みその　まき）

明治学院大学文学部英文学科卒業。同校在学中、カリフォルニア大学に留学。株式会社ディー・オー・エムでISOのコンサルティングや関連文書作成などを経て、現在、株式会社ディー・オー・エム・フロンティアに勤務。WebをベースとしたISOコンサルティングの開発、普及に携わっている。著書に、「会社の英語すぐに使える表現集」「英語論文すぐに使える表現集」「CDBOOK場面別会社で使う英会話」（ベレ出版）、「指で覚える　会社英語の基本の基本」「CDBOOK会社英語の基本ミニフレーズ1060」（明日香出版社）など。

## 小林知子（こばやし　ともこ）

高校時代をフランス・パリで過ごす。明治学院大学文学部フランス文学科卒業。卒業後、株式会社ディー・オー・エムを経て、現在、株式会社ディー・オー・エム・フロンティアに勤務。翻訳ビジネスに従事し、英語・フランス語を中心とした翻訳チェックを担当。その他、WebをベースとしたISOコンサルティング（e-Consulting）の制作や、CSR（企業の社会的責任）セミナーのコーディネータなどを務める。

## 英文校正　Darron Contryman

## ビジネスですぐに使えるEメール英語表現集

| | |
|---|---|
| 2003年 9 月25日 | 初版発行 |
| 2006年 6 月30日 | 第 9 刷発行 |

| | |
|---|---|
| 著者 | 株式会社ディー・オー・エム・フロンティア・味園真紀・小林知子 |
| カバーデザイン | 竹内雄二 |
| イラスト | 井ヶ田惠美 |

©DOM-Frontier 2003. Printed in Japan

| | |
|---|---|
| 発行者 | 内田　眞吾 |
| 発行・発売 | ベレ出版<br>〒162-0832 東京都新宿区岩戸町12　レベッカビル<br>TEL （03）5225-4790<br>FAX （03）5225-4795<br>ホームページ http://www.beret.co.jp/<br>振替 00180-7-104058 |
| 印刷 | 株式会社文昇堂 |
| 製本 | 根本製本株式会社 |

落丁本・乱丁本は小社編集部あてにお送りください。送料小社負担にてお取り替えします。

ISBN4-86064-034-9 C2082　　　　　　　　　　編集担当　脇山和美